The Composition of Fiscal Adjustment and Growth

Lessons from Fiscal Reforms in Eight Economies

G. A. Mackenzie, David W. H. Orsmond, and Philip R. Gerson

INTERNATIONAL MONETARY FUND
Washington DC
March 1997

Library of Congress Cataloging-in-Publication Data

Mackenzie, G.A. (George A.), 1950–
  The composition of fiscal adjustment and growth : lessons from fiscal reforms in eight economies / G.A. Mackenzie, David W.H. Orsmond, and Philip R. Gerson.
      p.   cm. — (Occasional paper, ISSN 0251-6365 ; 149)
  Includes bibliographic references.
  ISBN 1-55775-629-5
  1. Fiscal policy—Developing countries—Case studies.
2. Structural adjustment (Economic policy)—Developing countries—
Case studies.   3. Economic stabilization—Developing countries—
Case studies.   I. Orsmond, David William Harold, 1963– .
II. Gerson, Philip R.   III. Title.   IV. Series: Occasional paper (International Monetary Fund); no. 149.
HJ1620.M33   1997   96-30022
336.3′09172′4—dc21   CIP

Price: US$15.00
(US$12.00 to full-time faculty members and
students at universities and colleges)

Please send orders to:
International Monetary Fund, Publication Services
700 19th Street, N.W., Washington, D.C. 20431, U.S.A.
Tel.: (202) 623-7430   Telefax: (202) 623-7201
Internet: publications@imf.org

recycled paper

Contents

Boxes

Tables

Appendix

Figures

The following symbols have been used throughout this paper:

. . .   to indicate that data are not available;

—   to indicate that the figure is zero or less than half the final digit shown, or that the item does not exist;

–   between years or months (e.g., 1994–95 or January–June) to indicate the years or months covered, including the beginning and ending years or months;

/   between years (e.g., 1994/95) to indicate a crop or fiscal (financial) year.

"Billion" means a thousand million.

Minor discrepancies between constituent figures and totals are due to rounding.

The term "country," as used in this paper, does not in all cases refer to a territorial entity that is a state as understood by international law and practice; the term also covers some territorial entities that are not states, but for which statistical data are maintained and provided internationally on a separate and independent basis.

Preface

It is generally accepted that a stable financial environment is a prerequisite for sustainable economic growth. To set the stage for sustained growth, countries suffering from high inflation and balance of payments difficulties must pursue what can be a wrenching fiscal adjustment in order to resolve their external and internal disequilibria. The goals of fiscal policy, however, should go beyond simply reducing the size of the fiscal imbalance. The *way* in which the reduction in the deficit is achieved, or the *composition of fiscal adjustment,* is as important as the quantity of the adjustment. It has a critical bearing on the likelihood that adjustment efforts will be sustained, and on the impact of the adjustment on a country's long-run growth prospects. The importance of the "quality and composition of fiscal adjustment" was emphasized in the September 1996 "Declaration on Partnership for Sustainable Global Growth" of the Interim Committee (see IMF, 1996, page x).

This study, a companion to Occasional Paper 139, *Reinvigorating Growth in Developing Countries* (Goldsbrough and others, 1996), examines the composition of fiscal adjustment—the tax and expenditure policies and administrative procedures, and some aspects of public enterprise reform—in a sample of eight countries during a period usually of 15 years and ending in 1993. Its principal aim is to determine whether and to what extent the composition of fiscal adjustment in these countries can be said to have changed in a way that fostered growth over the adjustment period. One of the criteria the study uses in this assessment is the degree to which countries protected social expenditure—and expenditure on primary education and public and primary health care in particular.

The study is the product of a substantial collaborative effort by staff of the IMF's Fiscal Affairs Department. We are indebted to numerous colleagues for their assistance with the country analysis, in particular Juan Amieva, Etienne de Callatay, Dale Chua, James Daniel, Xavier Maret, Janet Stotsky, and Helga Treichel. We are also indebted to colleagues from the Tax Administration and Public Expenditure Management Divisions for their contributions. The statistical work was largely the responsibility of Scott Anderson and Chris Wu, and administrative support was ably provided by Pearl Acquaah, Randa Sab, and Ahwerah Vichailak. The authors also want to acknowledge the guidance and general support offered by Vito Tanzi, Teresa Ter-Minassian, and Peter Heller. Jim McEuen of the External Relations Department edited the paper for publication and coordinated production. The opinions expressed in the paper are those of the authors and do not necessarily reflect the views of the IMF or of its Executive Directors.

I Overview: Fiscal Reform and Economic Growth

Although the immediate objectives of IMF-supported programs are financial stabilization and a sustainable external position for the member country seeking IMF assistance, the ultimate aim is the improvement of living standards through increasing employment and economic growth.[1] The immediate objectives have proved more attainable, however, than this ultimate aim. A recent survey of the results of IMF-supported programs concluded that, although they were quite effective in reducing or eliminating macroeconomic imbalances—particularly external imbalances—they were less successful in achieving and sustaining higher rates of growth (Schadler and others, 1995).

The purpose of this study is to examine fiscal reforms in a group of eight countries—Bangladesh, Chile, Ghana, India, Mexico, Morocco, Senegal, and Thailand—during a recent period (usually 1978–93), in order to determine whether and to what degree the fiscal policies implemented during these adjustment efforts were supportive of growth. The study also explores why some countries enjoyed more success in this respect than others. The eight cases include both low- and middle-income countries, and countries with public sectors of varying sizes at the outset of the adjustment periods. The group includes countries forced to make a draconian adjustment to the fiscal stance in a crisis environment, but also countries whose adjustment efforts were more gradual. The analysis does not deal with the quantity of fiscal adjustment, as indicated by, for example, the magnitude of the decline in the primary deficit or other similar indicators. This and other macroeconomic aspects of the relationship between growth and adjustment are addressed in Occasional Paper 139, *Reinvigorating Growth in Developing Countries: Lessons from Adjustment Policies in Eight Countries* (Goldsbrough and others, 1996). Instead, this study provides a detailed exploration of the *composition* of the fiscal adjustment that was undertaken. It discusses reforms in expenditure policy, public expenditure management, tax policy and administration, and some aspects of public enterprise reform. Assessment of these policies is made with the aid of a stylized model of a growth-fostering public sector.

Characteristics of a Growth-Promoting Public Sector

The basic rule for a growth-promoting public sector is that its activities should complement, rather than compete with, those of the private sector. Thus, an important role is provided for the government in certain investments in human capital—particularly in primary education, public health, and basic health care—and in physical infrastructure. A certain level of expenditure on the legal system, public order, and civil administration is necessary to ensure a stable environment in which investments with long payoff periods will not be discouraged. Another basic rule is that the taxes that finance government expenditure should be as nondistortional as possible. To realize these expenditure and tax policies, a satisfactory level of organization and expertise in public administration is also necessary.

This study does not pretend to quantify exactly what the contribution of fiscal policy to actual growth has been in the eight countries examined.[2]

---

[1]Article I of the IMF's Articles of Agreement, which outlines the purposes by which "the Fund shall be guided in all its policies and decisions," speaks of "the promotion and maintenance of high levels of employment and real income" (Article I, Section (ii)).

[2]For example, it does not hazard statements such as "The change in the composition of social expenditures, improvements in public expenditure management, and reforms to the structure of the tax system and its administration in Chile added *x* percent to the annual rate of growth of real GDP in 1987–92." There simply is no existing model that would allow such inferences to be made. Although much valuable quantitative work has been done on the relationship between fiscal policy and growth, that work has stressed the macroeconomic dimension of fiscal policy, as in the impact of deficit financing on growth. When this analysis has considered the impact of particular components of fiscal policy, it has concentrated on a comparatively small number of expenditure categories. Changes in public expenditure management and tax administration, and in the complexities of tax and expenditure structure, are not modeled. These complexities and the likelihood of long lags between a change in policy and its impact on the economy are part of the reason why no general model has been developed.

Nonetheless, the model of the "growth-friendly" public sector described in Section II is grounded in the extensive theoretical and empirical literature on the nexus between fiscal policy and growth. The model is used in Section III as a basis for assessing the extent to which the fiscal reform policies implemented by the eight countries were conducive to growth.

Common Features of the Adjustment Experience

Generalizing from the different country experiences (details on the policies pursued by each country are provided in Appendices I, II, and III) Section III notes that one of the important common features of the developments in the eight countries is a tendency to achieve the greater part of the reduction in the primary deficit in the *initial* adjustment years. Moreover, in these years the main emphasis was on a reduction in noninterest expenditure; only in later years did the focus shift toward an increase in revenue. The initial expenditure cuts did not affect all types of expenditure equally; rather, most fell on current outlays on nonwage goods and services and on capital projects. Within these categories, the cuts were largely across-the-board and were not based on a systematic effort to minimize losses to productivity and growth. Expenditure on wages and salaries was generally protected, while outlays on subsidies and transfers fell gradually throughout the adjustment period.

Although a significant increase in revenue usually did not occur until late in the adjustment period, some reforms of the structure of the tax system were initiated in the first adjustment period. The most substantial tax reforms involved the replacement of a conventional sales tax by a value-added tax (VAT), which led in some cases to a broadening of the base of indirect taxation. The base of direct taxes was typically not broadened significantly.

Administrative reform, when it did occur, was more successful with tax administration than with public expenditure management. The most substantive reforms were undertaken by the countries that already had well-established basic systems in place before the adjustment efforts began; those countries where tax administration and public expenditure management were weak to begin with did **not** generally make major reforms to their administrative systems during the adjustment period. In some countries, these inadequacies hampered the successful implementation of expenditure and tax policy reforms, especially base-broadening measures such as the VAT.

Evaluating Whether Fiscal Reforms Promoted Growth

The model in Section II provides a basic standard of comparison that may be used in evaluating the extent to which fiscal reforms in the eight countries promoted growth. However, a meaningful evaluation has to take account of a country's starting point, as well as the constraints it faced as a result of its existing administrative and other systems, and the size of the quantitative fiscal adjustment it had to undertake. If no consideration were given to the initial impediments to high-quality adjustment, one might conclude that the initial adjustment was not optimal. However, the type of adjustment that *did* occur may have been necessary precisely because of the need to lay the administrative groundwork for a subsequent higher-quality adjustment. The following criteria embody both the desideratum of the model and these more practical considerations:

• the extent to which expenditures with a high social rate of return were protected and inefficient changes in the mix of expenditure avoided (in other words, the extent to which productive expenditure was maintained, despite the need for a decline in total expenditure);

• how quickly the countries started to address more fundamental issues in expenditure and public enterprise reform;

• how quickly they addressed basic tax reform issues; and

• how quickly administrative systems were reformed so as to support more efficient expenditure choices and better revenue-raising policies.

A brief summary of the individual country experiences shows that, among countries that made a major adjustment to their primary deficit, *Chile* stands out. It not only achieved a huge quantitative fiscal adjustment, it also dramatically transformed its public sector. Public expenditure was reduced, but the most productive expenditures were protected. The tax system was overhauled early in the adjustment effort: the need to rely on comparatively distortional taxes was lessened by the introduction of a broadly based VAT, and marginal effective rates of taxation of business income were substantially reduced. The public enterprise sector was drastically shrunk through privatization.

Mexico's reform was almost as broad in scope as Chile's, although it had difficulty maintaining the level of some productive expenditure during the adjustment efforts. *Morocco* had successes in various areas, although the size of the civil service remained excessive and progress in privatization was relatively limited.

Among the more moderate quantitative fiscal adjusters, *Thailand* also implemented some important reforms, although these were not as far reaching as those of Chile. Thailand's rapid growth allowed it to increase productive public expenditure, and distortional features of the tax system were reduced. *Ghana* made significant progress in expenditure policy and administrative reform, albeit from a low base. *Bangladesh* also made progress in reforming the tax structure. Much less progress was made by *India* in this area. In both India and Bangladesh, administrative deficiencies and problems with expenditure priorities remained largely unaddressed during the adjustment process, although India's adjustment efforts have only just begun. *Senegal*'s reform effort was largely unsuccessful in fostering a growth-oriented fiscal policy.

Lessons from Experience

Section IV draws lessons from the experiences of the eight countries in the implementation of their public sector reforms. In particular, the study suggests the following.

• Stabilization need not play havoc with a growth-friendly fiscal policy regime. It is possible to shelter most expenditures that exhibit a high social rate of return.

• Often there is a sequencing problem, where deficiencies in public expenditure management and tax administration initially require a rather crude approach to expenditure restraint and prevent the speedy reform of the tax system. Some expenditure cuts can, however, be damaging if not reversed in due course. To facilitate their reversal and to improve expenditure allocation, immediate action to reform both tax administration and public expenditure management is necessary. Whatever the pattern of expenditure reduction or tax increases initially adopted, structural reform will, for most countries, be an essential part of growth-oriented fiscal adjustment.

• The countries that either had basically good public expenditure management systems at the outset of the adjustment process or substantially improved a deficient system were more successful in protecting expenditure with a high social rate of return.

• Major reform of a tax policy regime requires either a reasonably well-functioning tax administration or a concurrent effort at administrative reform. At the same time, tax design must be cognizant of the limitations of tax administration.

• Substantial increases in revenue are possible without increases in average tax rates.

• Some basic structural reforms, such as civil service and enterprise reforms, important as they may be, cannot realize substantial budgetary saving in the short run. Reform in these areas should nonetheless start as soon as possible so as to achieve budgetary saving and to enhance growth prospects over the medium term.

The study also has the following implications for the design of adjustment programs.

• Given the crucial role of administrative reform in the successful implementation of tax and expenditure policy reform, there is a need for closer integration of improvements in tax administration and public expenditure management with basic program design at the outset of IMF-supported programs. However, a significant increase in the application of conditionality to administrative reforms is probably not feasible.[3]

• Tax policy measures are more easily made the object of conditionality than are measures of administrative reform. The application of conditionality to the composition of expenditure may, however, raise sensitive issues, which in some cases make it impracticable.

• More emphasis on the implications of fiscal adjustment for growth will require that increased attention be paid to the composition of expenditure.

• Similarly, IMF-supported programs should be sensitive to the risk that the initial heavy emphasis on expenditure restraint may become permanent and, by suppressing growth-fostering expenditure, may damage a country's growth prospects.

• A reorientation of social expenditure toward the primary levels (for example, primary education and public health and clinics) is doubly desirable: it yields positive effects on human capital formation and reinforces the social safety net, thus supporting the income and well-being of the poor.

• Certain reforms can entail, at least in principle, a trade-off between deficit reduction now and deficit reduction in the future, and this can be an issue when there is some flexibility in the timing of fiscal adjustment. Consequently, in the design of programs there is a need to view the budget increasingly in a multiperiod rather than a single-period framework.

---

[3]Conditionality refers to the policies that the IMF expects a country to follow in order to avail itself of IMF credit.

II How Fiscal Policy Can Affect Growth: Conceptual Issues and Evidence

A Basic Conceptual Framework[4]

Growth in actual output per person employed (productivity growth) can be attributed to one or more of the following sources:

• a more intensive utilization of existing productive capacity;

• a reallocation (more efficient use) of existing resources that reduces the gap between the economy's potential and actual output levels; and

• growth of the stocks of physical and human capital (relative to the growth of labor supply) or increased technological development.

The first two sources of productivity growth involve either more intensive or more efficient use of the existing stocks of the factors of production. They require some initial slack in the economy or the implementation of measures that reduce resource misallocation—for example, a well-conceived tariff reform or privatization program. The third source entails capital accumulation, whether physical or human, and thus can entail more than just short-lived increases in growth, unlike the first two.

The concern of this study is with the role of fiscal policy in stimulating the second and third sources of growth—especially the third, capital accumulation. Although economic theory provides a wealth of insights and a framework for thinking about growth, there are no conclusive rules that prescribe in any detail how to use fiscal policy to promote growth or that establish the relative importance of different fiscal policy measures. For example, although the optimal level of public investment in human and physical capital can be determined in principle, data deficiencies mean that calculating social rates of return on capital expenditure is generally not practicable.[5]

Nonetheless, the literature on economic growth, basic economic principles, and numerous empirical studies do offer some guidance on this question. Apart from pursuing a fiscal policy that is consistent with a low rate of inflation, an adequate amount of credit to the private sector, and a sustainable external position (that is, the macroeconomic aspects of fiscal policy), there are three ways in which the government can foster productivity growth:

• by either financing or supplying directly the investments that the private sector will not supply in adequate quantity because of various market failures (in practice, this means certain kinds of infrastructure projects and basic education and health expenditure, which can directly boost private sector productivity);[6]

• by efficiently supplying certain basic public services that are necessary to provide the basic conditions for entrepreneurial activity and long-term investment—that is, by minimizing the cost of producing a given volume of a public good or service; and

• by financing its own activities in a manner that minimizes distortions to private sector saving and investment decisions, and to economic activity more generally.

These policies contribute to growth by their impact on the level of output that can be achieved with existing capital stocks and human resources, by their direct contribution to capital formation, and by their effect on the private sector's decisions to save and invest, which contribute to capital accumulation. They are meant to be both growth enhancing and welfare enhancing.[7]

---

[4]This section's discussion of the literature on the role of fiscal policy in promoting growth is drawn from Gerson (forthcoming).

[5]Put simply, if the net present value of the income generated by a project exceeds the project's cost, using as the rate of discount the minimum rate of return a society expects of capital investments, the investment is socially profitable.

[6]Market failures stemming from the existence of imperfect capital markets and other sources can also justify the public provision of pensions. The effect on economic growth of public pension systems is a controversial matter. Theory suggests that pay-as-you-go schemes will depress saving and capital accumulation (Feldstein, 1974 and 1995). Empirical work gives some support, albeit not conclusive, for this view (Mackenzie and others, forthcoming).

[7]Growth-enhancing policies are not necessarily welfare enhancing. A policy of maximizing the rate of investment may increase growth at the expense of unduly burdening current generations: the current saving rate can be too high.

The rest of this section discusses in more detail the channels through which fiscal policy can affect growth—concentrating on its impact on capital accumulation—and summarizes the weight of the evidence of empirical studies. In addition, it deals with the importance of public administration for growth. Since some adjustment programs come to grief because fiscal measures cannot be sustained, it also discusses the sustainability of tax and expenditure measures.

Links Between Fiscal Policy and Growth

Investment in Physical and Human Capital[8]

Public Infrastructural Investment

Many infrastructural investments that can substantially increase the productivity of private sector activity cannot be undertaken profitably by the private sector, especially in countries without well-developed capital markets. These projects will be *complementary* to private sector investment, and *not competitive* with it. When projects have a social rate of return that is substantially higher than their private rate of return, there is a *prima facie* case for the state's involvement. The large initial outlays that certain investments require, and the problems that can arise in charging for their output, can justify public sector involvement. One example is investment in roads, where private ownership, even with regulated tolls, is not feasible in most cases. For investment in other areas, however, no obvious case for public ownership can be made beyond what is necessary for the basic functions of government.

A recent study (Easterly and Rebelo, 1993) of 119 countries found that public investment in transport and communication is positively related to growth, but that investment in public enterprises has no effect, and public investment in agriculture a negative effect, on growth. Other studies, mainly dealing with the states of the United States, have also found a positive relationship between infrastructural investment and growth. Although this finding is not common to all studies, the weight of the evidence offers moderate support for the view that infrastructural investment fosters growth, but that public investment in general does not (Gerson, forthcoming).

Educational Expenditure

Expenditure on education is potentially a highly productive investment, and its provision by the *public sector may be justified by market failures.* Education is typically both financed and supplied by the private sector to some extent. There are, however, reasons for thinking that the private sector, left to its own devices, would not provide enough education.

- Not all of the benefits of education accrue to the student alone, or, in the case of apprenticeships, to the employer financing the training; they may accrue also to the community at large and to subsequent employers.[9]
- The parents of school-age children, or students themselves, may discount the benefits of formal education excessively, particularly when the family is poor, because its opportunity cost (the out-of-pocket costs of education and the temporary decline in the student's productive time) appears to be too great.
- It is typically not possible to obtain a loan to pay for the substantial expense of a formal education.

The preceding discussion offers some clues about the relative merits of governmental involvement in primary and secondary education as opposed to tertiary education. The first two levels are those where the constraint imposed by imperfect credit markets is most severe, and the positive externality effects, and thus the effects on growth, are possibly the greatest, because of the importance to society of some of the skills taught.[10] For example, both basic literacy and numeracy are necessary for most jobs in a market economy and are associated with improved hygiene, better infant care, and lower birthrates (World Bank, 1990).

Many empirical studies of the relationship between education and growth have been made. Influential studies by Denison (1962, 1967), done at the aggregative level, implied that around 20 percent of the growth of U.S. GDP between 1930 and 1962 could be attributed to the increase in the workforce's educational level. A large number of studies of wage differentials between persons with different levels of education have found that schooling has a high rate

---

[8]International Monetary Fund (1995b) discusses some of the issues covered in this and the following subsections.

[9]There is an important parallel between expenditure on research and development and expenditure for on-the-job training, in that in neither case do the benefits of the expenditure accrue entirely to the enterprise that undertakes it. However, the return to research and development expenditure is typically highly uncertain, and the cost of the initial investment very high. Much of the benefit from research and development expenditure appears to be enjoyed not simply by other domestic firms, but by firms in other countries (Coe and Helpman, 1995). Thus, spending on research and development is not an attractive proposition for developing countries facing a severe public sector budget constraint.

[10]It is more difficult to borrow for primary and secondary education because of the longer period to maturity and greater riskiness of the loan. Even loans to tertiary level students in the United States under the Federal Student Loan program had a default rate of about 15 percent in 1994 (United States, 1995).

of return. Primary education is almost invariably found to have a higher return than secondary and tertiary education, even though in practice many developing countries subsidize the higher levels much more heavily than the primary level (Psacharopoulos, 1994).

Studies of the relationship between public spending on education (as opposed to the level of educational attainment) and growth are less clear-cut, perhaps because they typically aggregate education spending at all levels, and because they take little account of the long lag between the period of schooling and entry or reentry into the labor force. All in all, however, the literature supports the view that primary education deserves special emphasis, particularly in countries where literacy and primary school enrollment rates are low.

Health

Health care expenditure increases human productivity, and the positive externalities associated with preventive and primary care mean that public expenditure in these areas can promote growth. Clearly, expenditure on health, like education expenditure, can be an investment in human capital because it can prolong a person's productive life. As with education, the strongest case for intervention is in preventive and primary health expenditure (public health and clinics) because these expenditures either entail substantial externalities or have a very high social benefit-cost ratio. For example, it has been estimated that several of the most common diseases that afflict children in developing countries can be treated for only a few dollars per additional year of productive life gained (World Bank, 1993a). Because many people will not be able to afford even these comparatively simple treatments, the provision of free or subsidized treatment, by increasing productivity, can increase output, saving, and growth.[11] Certain public health interventions, such as well-designed immunization programs, are also highly cost-effective (World Bank, 1993a). As is the case for education, however, the empirical evidence linking aggregate public expenditure on health and growth is not strong. The weakness of the link may in part reflect that, in practice, much health expenditure is devoted to high-cost curative medicine.

The discussion of education and health expenditure is a good place to note that it is typically much easier to compare the rates of return of expenditure *within* a sector than it is to make comparisons across sectors. This is particularly true of the health sector, where it is evident that in many countries the rate of return to preventive care or simple curative techniques—as measured in lives saved or years of productive life gained—is far higher than costly care in hospitals.

Comparisons across sectors are far more problematic, mainly because of the difficulty of measuring social costs and benefits. That said, even if the social rate of return of additional kilometers of roads is difficult to compare with the rate of return from new schoolrooms, rough rules of thumb (and common sense) can be used to determine when there is a clear imbalance. A basically healthy population and a capital city with three-hour-long traffic jams do not suggest that the economic infrastructure budget should be cut to boost public health, for example.

Basic Public Services

Spending on the Social, Institutional, and Political Fabric

A certain level of expenditure by the state on the basic institutions of a market economy is necessary for growth. Growth is not generated automatically by the mere existence of capital and labor. The environment must not be hostile to economic activity, especially entrepreneurial activity, so that investment is not discouraged. Among other things, this normally requires a legal code and tax system that are both stable and administered fairly, respect for the rights of property, and physical security. It also requires a reasonably well-functioning public administration.[12]

There is clearly an empirical link between political or social stability and growth.[13] What is more difficult to ascertain is the role of government expenditure in this relationship. The maintenance of the social and institutional infrastructure that is necessary for a market economy requires some minimal amount of public expenditure on general public and tax administration, general regulatory activity, law and order, and, possibly, defense. Empirical studies have not found evidence, however, of a relationship between these expenditures and growth.

---

[11]The end of highly subsidized treatments for tuberculosis in China in the early 1980s is believed to have been the main factor behind a resurgence of the disease in the subsequent decade (World Bank, 1993a).

[12]These institutions are in any event essential for an organized, civil society.

[13]As one example, Alesina and others (1992) found that in a sample of 113 countries in 1950–82, those countries that had a high propensity for governmental collapse grew more slowly than those that did not. They also found evidence that instability causes lower growth, rather than vice versa.

Civil Service

A civil service promotes growth by delivering basic public services (and regulating economic activity) in an efficient and reliable way at a reasonable cost. Compensation and employment policy for an educated and well-motivated civil service would be based on the following principles.

• Civil service compensation should be comparable with that of the private sector (adjusting for security of employment and differences in other nonwage benefits of employment), with adequate salary differentials between different occupational groups within the civil service.

• Pay should be related to productivity, not personal or political connections, and promotion should be based on merit.

• Civil service employment should not be a tool of overall employment policy.

This is a description of a lofty ideal. Good pay policies alone will not eradicate corruption. Nonetheless, substantial deviations from these guidelines can do serious harm to a civil service's productivity, as well as burdening the budget (Haque and Sahay, 1996).

The Social Safety Net and Transfers to Persons and Enterprises

Spending on social assistance and other transfers to persons can foster growth to the extent that it reinforces the political viability of the policies and the environment necessary for growth. These expenditures are sometimes justified on the grounds that they help to alleviate poverty and prevent the fraying of the social fabric, thus reducing crime and other antisocial behavior that impedes productive economic activity.[14] There is some evidence of a positive link between transfer payments and growth (Cashin, 1995; and Sala-i-Martin, 1996).

Transfer payments, or possibly well-targeted commodity subsidies, can also serve to protect the vulnerable during adjustment. To the extent that such expenditure facilitates adjustment at a reasonable cost, it can thus be growth promoting. These expenditures and more permanent forms of social assistance can also promote growth by increasing the productivity of the poor. That said, social assistance and social safety net programs run the risk of encouraging overconsumption of the subsidized commodities and of making the effective marginal rate of taxation on welfare recipients so high that there is little incentive to seek work or keep a job (for a gen-

eral exposition of IMF policy on social issues, see IMF, 1995a).

It is more difficult to argue for operating subsidies to business enterprises.[15] As with untargeted general commodity subsidies, these can entail substantial distortions—in particular, inefficient and high-cost production techniques. One possible rationale for such operating subsidies is as a strictly temporary measure to facilitate restructuring or privatization; another is the need to cover losses resulting from production under conditions of decreasing marginal cost and marginal cost pricing.[16]

Financing Public Expenditure: The Tax System[17]

The effects of different tax regimes on the allocation of resources—in particular their effects on saving, investment, and labor supply—have been the topic of countless studies. Taxation creates distortions, essentially because it alters the relative prices of both final products and productive inputs so that they no longer reflect relative scarcities.[18]

The main object of tax policy is to design a system that raises enough revenue to meet a government's revenue target while minimizing the level of associated distortions.[19] Tax policy must also be mindful of the potential administrative complexity of a tax system, and of the burden of compliance imposed on the taxpayer. Its principal contributions to growth, aside from its contribution to macroeconomic stability, consist in minimizing the gap between actual and potential output—including its effect on the amount and allocation of work effort—and in minimizing the impediments to the productive investment of private saving.

---

[14]The provision of free or subsidized education to children from poor families may serve a similar function, in addition to its contribution to human capital formation.

[15]Operating subsidies are often funneled through the banking system, so that they do not show up in the accounts of the central government. This is especially true of economies in transition. More generally, the use of the central bank and other public financial institutions as a conduit for budgetary policy can entail substantial inefficiencies. This subject and related issues are addressed in Mackenzie and Stella (1996).

[16]These views are nicely encapsulated by the dictum "provide a social safety net for people, not firms."

[17]Although this subsection concentrates on taxes, nontax revenue is an important source of government revenue in some countries, especially property income (for example, transfers from public enterprises and the central bank). Further, certain fees and charges can serve an important allocative role—for example, toll charges for busy roads and bridges.

[18]There is an exception: some taxes can alleviate resource misallocation by increasing the effective price of goods whose market price does not reflect fully the social costs associated with their production or consumption. Such goods would include petroleum and tobacco products. However, taxes on these products would not by themselves raise enough revenue to finance even a minimal level of public expenditure.

[19]Tax policy can also be the servant of redistribution; for this, the personal income tax is normally the instrument of choice.

How the balance between these differing, and to some extent conflicting, objectives should be struck will vary from country to country, especially given the limits that may exist on administrative capacity. A consensus has emerged, however, that the "ideal" tax system for a developing country would have the following characteristics (Stotsky, 1995):

• heavy reliance on a broadly based sales tax, such as a VAT, preferably with a single rate and minimal exemptions, and excise taxes on petroleum products, alcohol, tobacco, and perhaps a few luxury items;

• no reliance on export duties, except possibly as a proxy for income tax for hard-to-tax sectors such as agriculture;

• reliance on import taxation for protective purposes only—since the domestic sales tax is assigned the revenue-raising function—with a low average rate and a limited dispersion of rates to minimize effective rates of protection;

• an administratively simple form of the personal income tax, with exemptions limited, if possible, to personal dependents' allowances, a moderate top marginal rate, an exemption limit large enough to exclude persons with modest incomes, and a substantial reliance on withholding; and

• a corporate income tax levied at only one moderate-to-low rate, with depreciation and other noncash expenditure provisions uniform across sectors, and minimal recourse to incentive schemes for new ventures.

Many of these features would be appropriate in both developing and industrial country settings. The special features of the tax system in the former are the lack of special emphasis on the personal income tax—an administratively demanding tax—and the emphasis on a simplified form of the VAT. The structure is seen as conducive to growth because, by striving for as broad a base and as uniform a rate structure as possible, it keeps top marginal rates down and avoids unnecessary rate differentiation.

The most likely channel through which taxation would affect growth is through its impact on saving and investment. As regards saving, the evidence suggests that tax regimes, by themselves, do not have a major impact on the *average level* of saving (Bovenberg and others, 1989; Smith, 1990; and Feldstein, 1994). There is considerable evidence, however, that the tax regime can affect the *allocation* of saving, mainly because not all forms of saving can be taxed equally. For example, it is generally easier to tax income from *financial* saving (that is, the accumulation of bank deposits, bonds, and shares) than income from *real* saving (investment in residential housing, art, and the like). One important consequence is that taxation of financial saving can promote financial disintermediation and excessive in-

vestment in real estate and other real assets. Because the income from financial assets is normally taxed without an adjustment for inflation, high rates of inflation can seriously exacerbate this distortion (Tanzi, 1984).

Studies of investment typically have found that it is moderately sensitive to a measure of the cost of capital, which is affected by the tax regime (Chirinko, 1993; and Mendoza, Milesi-Ferretti, and Asea, 1995). The tax regime is only one influence on the cost of capital, however, and the cost of capital only one influence on the investment decision. In the developing country setting, the evidence suggests that the effect of tax systems on investment is minimal. Other factors, such as political stability, play a more important role.[20]

Thus, the primary impact of fiscal policy on the level of investment may well originate on the expenditure rather than the revenue side of the budget. As with the saving decision, however, the tax regime has a greater influence on the *composition* of investment than on its level. In particular, when the structure of the corporate income tax varies across industries, because of, inter alia, differences in statutory rates or depreciation provisions, marginal effective rates of tax can vary substantially, which is highly distortional.[21] The distortional taxation of saving and investment can be expected to lower the average rate of return to investment, thereby reducing growth.

The tax regime can also affect the supply of labor. The size of this effect and that of the perverse effect of a tax transfer system, already noted, is limited within a developing country setting when income taxpayers are generally a small minority of the population. Nonetheless, excessive personal income tax rates undoubtedly contribute to the growth of the underground economy (Tanzi and Shome, 1993).

There is no extensive empirical literature on the allocative effects of sales taxation. A broadly based sales tax with uniform effective rates, such as the VAT, should nonetheless be preferable on allocational grounds to a tax with many different effective rates, such as a cascading turnover tax with an excise component that applies to a large number of goods (Harberger, 1988).[22] The extensive literature on tariffs and growth argues quite strongly for the view

---

[20]It is largely for this reason that investment incentives can entail a substantial loss in tax revenues without appreciably stimulating investment.

[21]Marginal effective rates of tax effectively adjust the statutory rate of tax on enterprises to take account of the impact on after-tax profitability of other aspects of the tax code, such as accelerated depreciation and loss carryovers (Chua, 1995).

[22]The theoretical literature supports the view that multiple rates may be optimal. In practice, however, it is not possible to estimate how rates should differ. Perhaps more important, multiple rates greatly increase administrative and compliance problems.

that, other things being equal, lower tariffs are good for growth.

Administration

Efficient tax administration and public expenditure management can reinforce the growth-promoting features of tax and expenditure policies. Conversely, expenditure policy, no matter how well designed, may see its intentions vitiated by bad public expenditure management. Good public expenditure management is a prerequisite for a competent evaluation of expenditure policies, for their effective execution, and for the timely monitoring of the budget. It is also essential to ensure that a change in the fiscal policy stance during the financial year can be effected in a way that minimizes the disruption to the most productive expenditure programs.

Good tax and customs administration gives a government more choice in designing a tax system, allowing it to rely on allocationally superior but administratively more demanding taxes. By ensuring that the tax system as actually administered coincides with the tax system of the statutes, good administration also contributes to the climate of stability and predictability that is a prerequisite for long-range investments and commercial activity. Efficient tax administration and public expenditure management also reduce the chance that a government's actual fiscal policy will prove incompatible with its macroeconomic targets.

Public Expenditure Management

The features of a growth-promoting public expenditure management system will differ from one country to another, if only because countries differ in their ability to apply complex systems. However, a well-functioning public expenditure management system would include, at a minimum, the following elements:

• use of a budget that integrates current and capital expenditure plans and relies on efficient appraisal techniques to decide among competing expenditure needs;

• utilization of aggregate expenditure ceilings, with effective control over expenditure during the year, coordination of domestic and foreign-financed expenditure, and effective management of cash and public debt; and

• a fiscal reporting system that compiles clear, reliable, comprehensive, and timely data on budget execution.

In a more advanced phase of development, the public expenditure management system would imbed the budgetary process in a medium-term macroeconomic framework. In its most sophisti-cated form, such a multiyear approach would include the following elements:

• a medium-term fiscal policy forecasting model;

• rolling forward cost estimates of continuing programs; and

• a disciplined procedure for adding new programs to the forward estimates.

These more advanced forms of public expenditure management require considerable capacity for forecasting and analysis of short- and medium-term budget trends and priorities. They could be included, either in whole or in part, in the public expenditure management procedures of a country that had largely mastered the more fundamental procedures just described.

The final—and most advanced—phase involves the use of performance-based accountability to improve efficiency in the public sector through an allocation of resources that is more closely in line with local needs and conditions. In particular, in several advanced countries there has been a trend toward a decentralization of management authority to meet specified objectives within an (overall) budgetary ceiling.[23] A reliable and accurate flow of data back to the center to maintain accountability is a critical component of this approach.

Tax Administration

The basic ingredients of a sound tax administration are as follows:

• reliance, where feasible, on voluntary compliance and self-assessment, entailing, among other things, adequate education of taxpayers, simple forms and instructions, and simplified filing and payment procedures;

• use, where possible, of final withholding;

• efficient detection procedures for delinquent taxpayers, requiring an up-to-date and accurate taxpayer registration system that can detect "stopfilers" and delinquent taxpayers;

• efficient and impartial enforcement and collection procedures (among them, the issuing of notices), including a system of penalties that maximizes the incentive to comply, together with simple procedures for the settlement of disputes; and

• reliance on systematic audit plans and procedures (for example, the number of companies that

---

[23]For example, in New Zealand, chief executives of government departments are appointed for five years on a performance-based contract. They are free of almost all controls over budget inputs and thus enjoy the right to buy and sell their assets, to hire and fire, and to set salaries. The Auditor-General checks whether the services agreed were delivered, and the departments' efficiency and effectiveness are regularly compared against other departments and the private sector (New Zealand, 1993).

will be audited each year), with use of single-issue and in-depth audits, modern information systems to select taxpayers for audit, and employment of qualified audit personnel.

The organization and procedures of an efficient system would have the following two basic features:

• organization along functional lines (collection, enforcement, taxpayer education)—rather than by type of tax—to facilitate staff specialization and eliminate duplication and inefficiencies; and

• reliance on the computer for clerical tasks, when justified by the number of taxpayers.

It is worth reemphasizing that tax system design must take into account both the administrative capacity of the tax department and the burden of compliance that the system imposes on taxpayers.

Sustainability

The introduction of sustainability as a criterion for the choice of fiscal measures adds an extra dimension to the analysis. Normally, fiscal sustainability refers to the notion that a given fiscal stance is compatible with a level of public debt to GDP that can be serviced without difficulty and without entailing an unsustainable buildup in either internal or external debt. But there is another important sense in which fiscal policy can be unsustainable: when it relies on cuts in expenditure or increases in revenue that cannot be maintained indefinitely. Although a stabilization program must sometimes rely initially on such unsustainable measures, eventually they will have to be replaced by measures that can be sustained (Tanzi, 1989).[24]

There are two principal reasons to think that sustainable measures are a sine qua non for growth. First, if adjustment cannot be sustained, internal and external stability will not be achieved. Second, unsustainable policies imply that there will be changes in policy regimes. For example, countries prone to high inflation and facing unstable debt dynamics may be tempted to adopt policies that impose what amount to confiscatory tax rates on holders of public debt; real interest rates then will be prone to substantial fluctuations; and fluctuations in aggregate output may be exaggerated. These conditions are inimical to the kind of stable policy environment in which investment and long-range planning can thrive.[25]

The question then arises whether there is a conflict between those fiscal measures that promote growth and those that are sustainable. This cannot be answered from first principles. Experience suggests, however, that the conflict may be minimal. Indeed, it is often the stopgap measures that are unsustainable, since they do not offer satisfactory solutions to more basic underlying problems.[26]

• The short-run fiscal consequences of an overstaffed civil service—an increasing share of the wage bill in expenditure—are often addressed by an across-the-board wage freeze. Quite apart from the fact that such freezes will generally be reversed, they do not attack the basic problem—excess employment—and probably reduce public sector efficiency by lowering salaries and compressing salary scale differentials.

• Across-the-board expenditure cuts or freezes, affecting all functional and economic expenditure categories, may be easy to implement but are clearly inefficient. They are less likely to lead to the permanent reduction in expenditure that results when specific programs are cut.

• Increased statutory tax rates on an existing tax base can be quickly implemented but, if the rates are already high, can cause erosion of the tax base and increase distortions.

---

[24]Unsustainable measures may not have to be replaced if the initial target for the deficit is below its long-run target; they can be phased out. See Alesina and Perotti (1996) and McDermott and Wescott (1996) for empirical applications of this aspect of sustainability to OECD countries.

[25]There is a link between low growth and macroeconomic instability; see Goldsbrough and others (1996).

[26]One possible exception to this rule is a reduction in the investment budget. As noted earlier, however, cutbacks in investment may not have much impact on growth if cuts fall on projects with a low rate of return. In any case, the cuts may be easier to sustain politically than cuts in unproductive current expenditure—such as ill-targeted commodity subsidies—that have powerful political constituencies.

III Country Experiences with Public Sector Reform

The objective of this section is to assess the growth-fostering characteristics of the public sector reforms undertaken by eight countries during a period normally of about 15 years (usually 1978–93). Section II sketched the outlines of a growth-promoting public sector. However, a sketch of the final destination or target of economic policy cannot necessarily serve as a road map that explains how to get there. In interpreting the actual policies implemented by the eight countries, one must recognize that, even if growth were the paramount policy objective, all the countries faced institutional constraints that limited their ability, at least in the short run, to pursue a growth-oriented fiscal policy.

These constraints are examined below, and some basic features of the adjustment common to the eight countries are set out. The section then appraises the growth-promoting character of the public sector reforms adopted by each of the eight countries (using the model in Section II), while at the same time taking into account the constraints the countries faced.

To speak first of methodology, for each country, the period under review is divided into three subperiods: a preadjustment period and two subsequent adjustment periods. The latter two periods can be distinguished by the intensity and type of fiscal (and other) reform efforts undertaken (Table 1).[27] The adjustment periods tend to be about six years long and were selected to coincide with a substantial adjustment effort, often prompted by a balance of payments crisis. Each country's adjustment efforts were supported by at least one arrangement with the IMF.

The analysis here is concerned mainly with developments at the central government level; where possible, the study uses data on the financial operations of the consolidated central government.[28] It also deals

---

[27]These periods are similar to those used in Goldsbrough and others (1996). In Chile's case the preadjustment period begins in 1972 and the second adjustment period ends in 1989. Some structural reform did take place in the years that followed, which is covered by the study. In Ghana, expenditure increased rapidly in 1992, which contributed to a marked increase in the primary deficit after the end of the second adjustment period. Since then, expenditure has been contained, and revenue has been relatively buoyant, so that the primary deficit has shrunk. India has had only one adjustment period, starting from 1991. Finally, Thailand undertook an adjustment effort during 1981–86 with IMF assistance; during 1987–93 there was no IMF-supported program, but several important fiscal policy changes were introduced, and the period is characterized here as a second adjustment phase.

[28]Focusing on central government, rather than on general government or the nonfinancial public sector, has the advantage that taxing, spending, and financing decisions at this level are basically under the control of the central government. In any case, general government and public sector data are not available in

---

Table 1. Designation of "Adjustment Periods"

Country	Preadjustment	Adjustment I	Adjustment II
Bangladesh	1978/79–1979/80	1980/81–1984/85	1985/86–1993/94
Chile	1972–73	1974–82	1983–89
Ghana	1978–82	1983–86	1987–91
India	1978/79–1990/91	1991/92–1992/93	
Mexico	1978–1982	1983–87	1988–93
Morocco	1978–80	1981–85	1986–93
Senegal	1979/80–1982/83	1983/84–1987/88	1988/89–1993
Thailand	1978–80	1981–86	1987–93

Box 1. Overview of Adjustment in the Eight Countries

Bangladesh. After an extended period in the 1970s of political turmoil, heavy government intervention in the economy, and poor growth performance, the government initiated an ambitious growth-oriented strategy in 1979. This strategy targeted increased saving and investment combined with extensive structural reforms; in the event, these targets were missed by wide margins on account of adverse shocks and policy slippages, so that macroeconomic imbalances continued to increase. A second phase of adjustment started in the mid-1980s; the combination of fiscal tightening and structural reforms, in particular unification of the foreign exchange market and trade liberalization, succeeded in reducing inflation and improving the external current account. Real per capita GDP growth remained low, however, reflecting continuing serious structural distortions.

Chile. A large drop in output in 1973 accompanied by hyperinflation led to the adoption of an economic program in 1974–75 involving a sharp tightening of fiscal policy, large corrective price increases, a flexible exchange rate policy, and significant structural reforms, including a reversal of the previous expropriation of enterprises. Aiming to reduce inflation to world levels, the government fixed the exchange rate in mid-1979, but the inconsistency of this policy with wage indexation and ongoing inflation in nontradables led to a sharp real effective appreciation of the peso and a boom in consumption and imports financed by large external borrowing, accompanied by lax control of banking activity. A drop in the price of copper and an abrupt decline in access to external financing in the wake of the debt crisis led to a severe recession and a banking crisis in 1982–83. The medium-term stabilization and adjustment program adopted in 1983 included a flexible exchange rate, eliminating mandatory wage indexation, restoring the financial system, and reducing

the fiscal deficit. Further privatization of public enterprises was carried out, and there was a major reform of the social security system. Since 1985, Chile has enjoyed strong economic growth.

Ghana. The Economic Recovery Program (ERP) introduced in 1983 followed a protracted period of economic decline caused by massively interventionist policies, widespread price controls and exchange restrictions, and a large decline in the terms of trade. The first phase of the ERP (1983–86)—based on restrained financial policies, elimination of widespread domestic price controls and other regulatory restrictions, and large devaluations to correct a severely overvalued exchange rate—succeeded in eliminating the most severe macroeconomic imbalances. At the same time, a resumption of official external financing supported a pickup in public investment. The second phase (1987–91) completed the comprehensive liberalization of the trade and exchange system and featured a reform of the financial system as well as more vigorous efforts to restructure and privatize a large public enterprise sector (see Hadjimichael and others, 1996).

India. In the second half of the 1980s, expansionary fiscal policies, including stepped-up public investment, brought about some pickup in growth but also contributed to wider external current account deficits and rising external debt. Shocks to the balance of payments, associated with the 1990 Middle East crisis, and internal political problems triggered an outflow of capital and a major liquidity crisis in early 1991. The new government responded by depreciating the rupee, raising interest rates, cutting the public sector deficit, and implementing significant, but incomplete, structural reforms—most notably industrial deregulation, partial trade liberalization, and an opening up to foreign in-

---

with some aspects of reforms undertaken in the public enterprise sector, mainly with a view to assessing their impact on the central government's budget.

sufficient detail over an extended period for most of the eight countries. Fortunately, local government is a small share of total general government expenditure in the countries under consideration (with the exception of India), and hence focusing on fiscal adjustments at the central government level is not overly restrictive. The data reported for education and health expenditure in India, however, are for general government, since the state governments account for the lion's share of this type of expenditure. In Mexico's case, oil royalties have been included with taxes paid by Pemex, the state oil company, instead of being included in nontax revenues. Expenditures in the early 1980s reflect the costs incurred by the government in winding up the Mexdollar scheme. It should also be noted that discussions of Mexican fiscal policy generally rely on a broader measure of public sector operations than the federal government.

Initial Constraints and Pattern of Adjustment

Initial Conditions

At the outset of adjustment, all eight countries were experiencing macroeconomic imbalances of varying degrees of severity (Box 1). The need for substantial *fiscal* adjustment was evident because the primary deficit—the difference between noninterest expenditure and revenue—averaged 6.0 percent of GDP (varying from 3.7 percent in Ghana to 10.2 percent in Bangladesh).

There were signs of serious structural problems as well. In *Bangladesh, Ghana,* and *India,* deficiencies in tax administration had contributed to a heavy reliance on taxes that are comparatively simple to ad-

vestment. In response, the balance of payments position strengthened substantially during 1992–94, aided by capital inflows (see Chopra and others, 1996).

Mexico. After the 1982 debt crisis and a cutoff from external financing, Mexico introduced an adjustment strategy based on fiscal tightening, frequent adjustments of the exchange rate, some moderate privatization, and, after 1985, trade liberalization. Inflation remained high, however, and growth and private investment stagnated. A new disinflation strategy, introduced in December 1987, was based on further fiscal tightening and the use of the exchange rate as the main nominal anchor supported by income policy agreements between labor, business, and the government. Together with a successful restructuring of external debt, this strategy slowed inflation and paved the way for a resumption of access to international financial markets, and a surge of capital inflows. However, the real exchange rate appreciated, private saving declined sharply, and a large external current account deficit emerged, leading eventually to a new crisis in late 1994.

Morocco. During the 1970s, expansionary financial policies—prompted by the 1974 phosphate boom—resulted in large fiscal and external current account deficits and a rapid buildup of external debt. These imbalances added to a wide range of structural weaknesses. A succession of adverse exogenous shocks critically weakened the external position, leading to debt-servicing difficulties by the early 1980s. The subsequent adjustment strategy had several phases: through 1985, the emphasis was on fiscal adjustment through large cuts in capital expenditure (with most of the adjustment occurring in 1983–85), tight monetary policy, and active exchange rate policy to improve competitiveness; the next phase (1986–93) emphasized greater

trade liberalization and deregulation, extensive tax reforms, financial market reform, and reforms of pricing policies and state enterprises. In this phase, the nominal exchange rate was anchored to a currency basket, apart from small step devaluations in 1990 and 1992.

Senegal. During the late 1970s and early 1980s, a succession of droughts, deterioration of the terms of trade, and inappropriate policies resulted in large fiscal and external current account deficits and a rising external debt. After a period of unsuccessful stabilization efforts, sustained adjustment was achieved during 1983–88, founded on significant fiscal consolidation and structural reforms. Together with more favorable terms of trade and weather conditions, this led to an improved economic performance. But the gains were not long-lasting: in 1989–93, financial policies weakened, structural reform stalled, and external competitiveness continued to deteriorate in the face of adverse terms of trade shocks. In early 1994, adjustment efforts were renewed, and the CFA franc was devalued by 50 percent (see Hadjimichael and others, 1996).

Thailand. The expansionary public sector policies of the late 1970s resulted in growing fiscal and external imbalances and left the Thai economy in a vulnerable position when it was hit with the external shocks of 1980–82. Following a brief period when adjustment measures produced only marginal improvements, a major adjustment effort was undertaken in 1984–85, when the baht was devalued, significant fiscal consolidation began, and a decisive change was made in the orientation of trade and industrial policies toward export-led growth. Since 1987, Thailand has been in the midst of an investment- and export-led economic boom with large accompanying capital inflows (see Kochhar and others, 1996).

minister—specific excise and international trade taxes—rather than on more broadly based—and allocationally efficient—taxes.[29] Effective tax rates were high, mainly to compensate for the narrow base of the system, a problem aggravated in India and Bangladesh by the impact of numerous ad hoc exemptions and preferences. These and other features of the tax system complicated its administration and created distortions. Further, the low revenue yield limited the opportunity of these countries to under-

take necessary productive expenditure, and weak public expenditure management—and inefficient public sector enterprises—led to wasteful subsidies and diminished the productivity of the expenditure that could be financed. Education and health expenditures were low overall and did not emphasize the primary level sufficiently, so that a large part of the populace was without even basic medical care. In addition, consumer subsidies for basic foodstuffs and other goods were not well targeted.

The public sector in some of the other countries during the preadjustment period had similar features. A weak tax administration in *Senegal* contributed to a heavy reliance on international trade taxes, although an effort had been taken to broaden the tax base with the introduction of a VAT. Expenditure was high, in part because of excessive salaries and

---

[29]In Ghana, a vastly overvalued exchange rate also lowered the yield from taxes on tradable goods. In India, dependence on trade and excise taxes was encouraged by the constitutional provisions that exempt trade tax revenue from the revenue-sharing arrangements between the center and the states and give jurisdiction over sales taxes to the states.

employment in the civil service and because of high but relatively unproductive capital expenditure. In *Mexico* a large public enterprise sector, despite being protected by substantial tariff and nontariff barriers, was proving to be a significant drain on the budget. Although a VAT had been introduced, its structure made it difficult to administer. The base of the system as a whole was not as broad as it could be, and evasion was a serious problem.

Morocco's expenditure was inflated at the outset of the first adjustment period, having increased following the phosphate boom in the early 1970s but not having declined when the terms of trade deteriorated after 1975. Ad hoc tax exemptions and high import tariffs further complicated a complex tax system that suffered from low revenue elasticity and hampered tax administration. Weaknesses in budget programming and monitoring, especially of capital expenditure, contributed to the public sector's structural deficiencies.

In *Chile,* a deterioration in the terms of trade exacerbated a weak fiscal position. High rates of inflation eroded the ratio of revenue to GDP, and the ratio of expenditure to GDP was high. Import restrictions had proliferated, and the nationalization of most industrial enterprises entailed a drain on the budget because of the subsidies required.

Finally, in *Thailand,* defense and other expenditure had been stepped up in the preadjustment period. The tax base had eroded through extensive reliance on exemptions, and the main sales tax was highly cascaded. Import tariffs were numerous and often specific, and they entailed fairly high average effective rates of protection. That said, Thailand did not have structural problems as severe as some of the other countries.

Quantity and Pattern of Adjustment

Quantitative Adjustment

All countries reduced the size of their primary deficit over the two adjustment periods combined (Table 2; Figures 1, 2, and 3); the average decline was 6.1 percent of GDP. The largest declines were recorded in the countries that began their adjustment efforts with the largest primary deficits (Bangladesh, Chile, Mexico, and Morocco). More than half of the average decline of 4 percent of GDP occurred during the first adjustment period, reflecting the emphasis initially placed in some countries on restoring macroeconomic stability.[30]

The relative emphasis of the adjustment effort on expenditure or revenue measures changed over time. The adjustments in the *first period* were principally undertaken through a reduction in noninterest expenditure (which declined by an average of 3 percent of GDP, compared with an average increase in revenue of just 1 percent).[31] In contrast, the reductions in the primary deficit (for some countries, increases in the primary surplus) in the *second period* relied more on increasing the revenue share in GDP and less on cuts in expenditure, Chile being the exception.[32] The largest decreases in the share of noninterest expenditure in GDP during the adjustment efforts were in the countries that initially had the highest ratios of expenditure to GDP (Chile, Mexico, Morocco, and Senegal). In contrast, countries with a low initial ratio of revenue to GDP were not necessarily the ones that had a large increase in the revenue share.

Pattern of Adjustment

The adjustments made to **each of the components** of fiscal policy and administration are summarized in Box 2, which draws heavily on the detailed and more country-specific accounts of the public sector reforms presented in Appendix I.[33] This summary indicates that, taking the adjustment period as a whole, there are some clear differences in the quality of the fiscal adjustment undertaken in the eight countries. However, the data also suggest a fairly common pattern of adjustment in the early years.

As noted previously, noninterest expenditure typically bore the brunt of adjustment, especially during the first adjustment period. A greater contribution from the revenue side could, in principle, have been had by implementing one or more of three changes to the tax structure:
- increasing the rates of existing taxes;
- widening the base of existing taxes; and
- introducing new and more broadly based taxes.

The first option was unlikely to raise significant revenue, since tax rates were already high and prob-

---

[30]In Chile, Ghana, Morocco, and Thailand the decline was greater in the second period than in the first.

[31]The exception was Ghana, which started with the lowest expenditure and revenue shares, and where both expenditure and revenue increased.

[32]In Chile, the expenditure and revenue shares of GDP experienced a very pronounced decline during the second adjustment phase. In the other countries, revenue increased on average by 1.8 percent of GDP, while expenditure remained fairly flat. Revenue is, however, more sensitive to external factors than domestic expenditure, and the revenue trends during the second adjustment period as well as the first may have at least partly reflected favorable developments in the terms of trade rather than discretionary policy measures.

[33]Appendix I is organized on a "topical" basis, in order to facilitate comparison of the different elements of expenditure and tax policy and administration across the eight countries.

Table 2. Summary of Adjustment Efforts
(In percentage points of GDP)

Country	Level		Change[1]		
	Initial	End of period	Overall	Adj. I	Adj. II
			Primary balance		
Bangladesh	−10.2	−4.6	5.6	3.8	1.8
Chile	−6.1	2.2	8.3	2.0	6.3
Ghana	−3.7	−2.6	1.1	0.4	0.8
India	−4.5	−1.7	2.8	2.8	...
Mexico	−6.7	3.4	10.0	10.0	—
Morocco	−7.8	3.0	10.7	4.4	6.4
Senegal	−5.6	−1.8	3.8	6.3	−2.5
Thailand	−3.8	2.9	6.7	2.2	4.5
Average	−6.0	0.1	6.1	4.0	2.5
			Noninterest expenditure		
Bangladesh	18.8	15.9	−2.9	−3.8	0.9
Chile	34.9	19.2	−15.7	−1.3	−14.4
Ghana	9.7	16.3	6.6	7.2	−0.6
India	18.0	15.9	−2.1	−2.1	...
Mexico[2]	22.4	13.7	−8.7	−8.6	−0.1
Morocco	29.9	23.9	−6.0	−5.8	−0.2
Senegal	24.6	18.0	−6.6	−7.7	1.1
Thailand	18.8	15.6	−3.1	−1.6	−1.5
Average	22.1	17.3	−4.8	−3.0	−2.1
			Revenue[3]		
Bangladesh	8.6	11.3	2.6	−0.1	2.7
Chile	28.8	21.4	−7.4	0.7	−8.1
Ghana	6.0	13.8	7.7	7.6	0.1
India	13.5	14.2	0.7	0.7	...
Mexico	15.7	17.0	1.3	1.4	−0.1
Morocco	22.1	26.8	4.7	−1.4	6.2
Senegal	19.0	16.1	−2.8	−1.4	−1.4
Thailand	14.9	18.5	3.6	0.6	3.0
Average	16.1	17.4	1.3	1.0	0.3

Sources: IMF, *Government Finance Statistics Yearbook* (various issues); and various IMF Staff Country Reports.
[1]Positive figures represent improvements in the primary balance.
[2]Includes exchange rate subsidies between 1982–87.
[3]Excluding grants.

ably quite distortional.[34] The possibility that the second option could raise significant amounts of revenue was limited by the difficulty of taxing agricul-

ture and services, and by the increased cascading that broadening the base of the existing sales tax would entail.

This left the third option—introducing new and more broadly based taxes, such as the VAT. Mexico and Senegal had already introduced a VAT; and Chile introduced a VAT early in the first adjustment period. Although Chile experienced a substantial increase in sales tax receipts (5 percent of GDP), the increase in Mexico and Senegal was more modest; the differences can be explained in part by the simplicity of design of the Chilean VAT and the compar-

---

[34]One exception to this generalization for some countries was the imposition of a tax or an increase in the rates of existing taxes on basic excisable goods such as petroleum; this path was followed in Morocco and Ghana, but not until several years into the adjustment efforts. Another option for base broadening was the elimination of corporate tax incentive schemes. This measure would not raise significant revenue, at least in the short term, since such measures would have been difficult to apply retroactively.

Figure 1. Primary Balance
(In percent of GDP)[1]

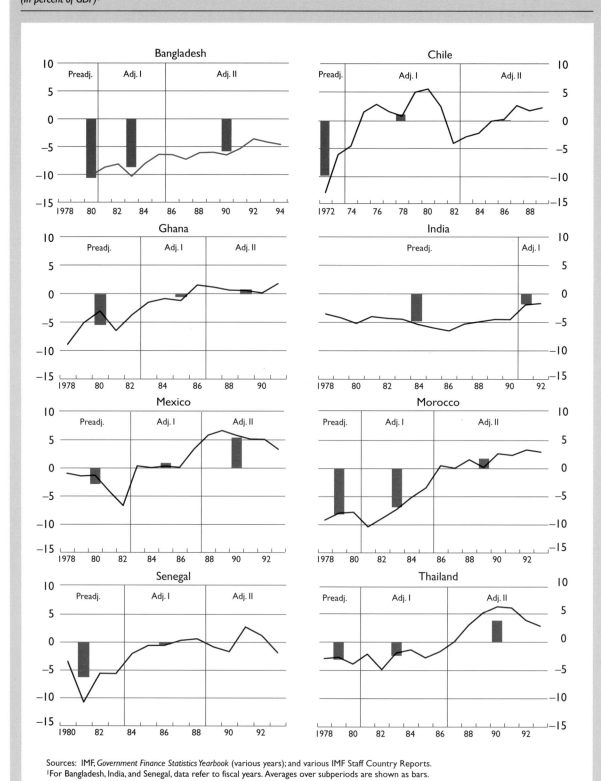

Sources: IMF, *Government Finance Statistics Yearbook* (various years); and various IMF Staff Country Reports.
[1]For Bangladesh, India, and Senegal, data refer to fiscal years. Averages over subperiods are shown as bars.

Figure 2. Expenditure Excluding Interest Payments
(In percent of GDP)[1]

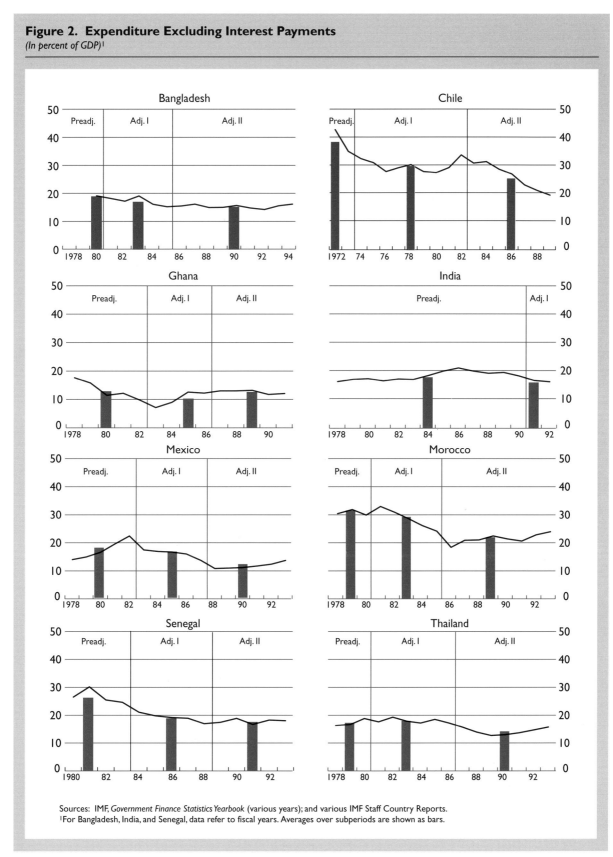

Sources: IMF, *Government Finance Statistics Yearbook* (various years); and various IMF Staff Country Reports.
[1]For Bangladesh, India, and Senegal, data refer to fiscal years. Averages over subperiods are shown as bars.

Figure 3.   Total Revenue Excluding Grants
(In percent of GDP)[1]

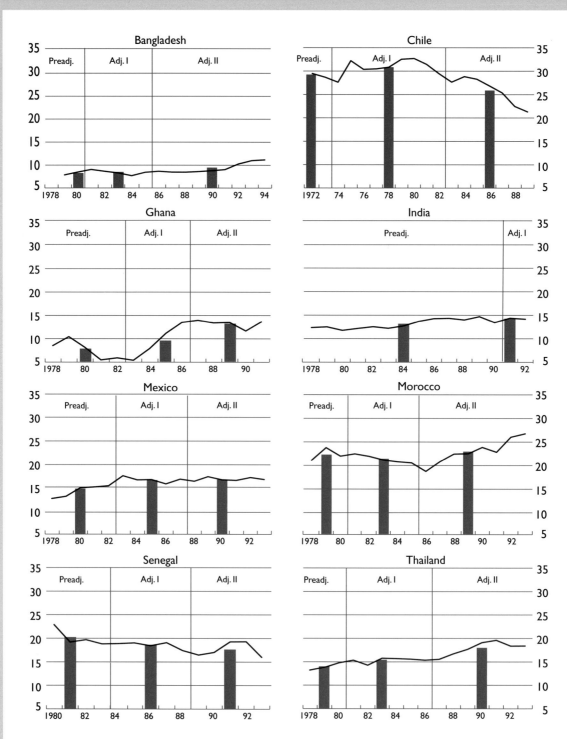

Sources: IMF, *Government Finance Statistics Yearbook* (various years); and various IMF Staff Country Reports.
[1]For Bangladesh, India, and Senegal, data refer to fiscal years. Averages over subperiods are shown as bars.

ative efficiency of Chile's tax department. For various reasons—including the complex preparations necessary for the successful introduction of a VAT—none of the five remaining countries introduced a VAT during the first adjustment period. Of these countries, only Ghana substantially increased revenue in the first adjustment period, and this was mainly attributable to the effect of the exchange rate devaluation on customs, export, and excise tax receipts rather than to fundamental tax reform.

The limited scope for increasing revenue explains why the bulk of the adjustment in the first period fell on noninterest expenditure. These expenditure cutbacks were not usually spread equally across all economic categories. In particular, the scope for quick but substantial and lasting reductions in the civil service wage bill was limited (Figure 4). Wage freezes were commonly tried, only to be at least partially reversed subsequently. Hiring freezes were also ineffective. The lack of success and unsustainability of these policies stemmed in part from the difficulties they created for efforts to fill senior and professional positions in the civil service. Employment reductions would prove expensive at the outset because of the need to make severance payments. A policy to reduce employment at the unskilled level, combined with increased pay and employment for skilled workers, was the most growth-enhancing approach (and was followed in Chile toward the end of the first adjustment period and in Ghana during the second).

Some success was achieved in cutting back subsidies and transfers; better targeting of consumer subsidies toward the poor contributed to this result. Similarly, transfers to enterprises could be decreased through adjustment of their tariffs, with an associated decrease in the degree of distortion to relative prices. Reduced transfers to enterprises made possible by efficiency gains, however, typically took considerable time and could not be relied on for substantial budgetary saving, at least in the short run (Table 3 and Figure 5).

Given these rigidities and the need to realize quickly the required level of budgetary saving, two vulnerable forms of expenditure were cut by virtually all countries: expenditure on other current goods and services, and capital expenditure (Figures 6 and 7). These cuts would not have much impact on a country's growth prospects if the expenditures eliminated were wasteful (had a low rate of return). That said, a decline large enough to cut deeply into productive capital expenditure would eventually reduce medium-term growth prospects if slow progress in fiscal reform meant that these reductions could not be reversed. Similarly, over time an inadequate level of operation and maintenance expenditure would rapidly reduce the productivity of the public capital stock, while cuts in other goods

and services expenditure would contribute to a growing imbalance between labor and materials and supplies.

Establishing Criteria for Assessing the Growth-Fostering Character of Fiscal Policies

In light of the impediments that countries confronted in their efforts to reform the public sector, and their different starting points, it would not be sensible to judge a country's efforts on the basis of how close it had come, by the end of the adjustment period, to some ideal or model of a growth-fostering public sector. Instead, a country's efforts should be judged by the direction that reform took, by the depth of reforms, and by the degree to which reforms were implemented in the right sequence. The growth-enhancing nature of a country's adjustment efforts would depend considerably on how quickly it was able to undertake reforms that could counteract the effects of the initial cuts in expenditure on capital and other goods and services. More generally, a country's efforts would be judged on the basis of how far they took the economy down the road to the ideal. The countries with the best growth adjustment profile, then, would be those that, from the start of the adjustment process:

• reallocated expenditure priorities toward, or at least preserved, the most productive areas, especially for operation and maintenance and within the capital budget;

• minimized reliance on indiscriminate expenditure cuts across broad expenditure categories such as other current goods and services, which would typically prove to be temporary;

• took early action to reform the tax system;

• strengthened expenditure and tax administration so as to improve the efficiency of expenditure, increase the tax yield over time, and allow for the adoption of a less distortive tax system; and

• undertook reform of public enterprises to eliminate uneconomic subsidies and increase the enterprises' operational efficiency.

Assessing the Growth Conduciveness of Public Sector Reform

To some extent, all the countries adopted policies along the lines described above. There are, nonetheless, striking differences among them. For a variety of reasons—most important, the influence of other macroeconomic and structural policies, and the lags between public expenditure on human and physical capital and its effect on output—these differences cannot be said to "explain" differences in the countries' actual growth performances during the adjust-

Box 2. Overview by Type of Fiscal Component

Expenditure

Directly Productive Expenditure. The share of total education expenditure in GDP decreased in some countries during the adjustment period, but the declines were proportionately less than that for total noninterest expenditure. Of particular importance from the growth perspective, in Chile and Thailand, primary education standards were protected and improved. This was not the case in most of the other countries.

The trends in health expenditure were similar to those in education. The share of total health expenditure in GDP was not substantially reduced during the adjustment efforts, despite the decrease in total noninterest expenditure. Although in general there was some improvement in primary care, the countries with the poorest health indicators at the outset of the adjustment efforts—such as Bangladesh, Ghana, and Senegal—were not those that made the most progress in increasing the focus on primary health expenditure.

Government investment often experienced a disproportionately large share of the expenditure adjustment effort, especially during the initial years. Chile, Ghana, Morocco, and Thailand appear to have best preserved investment in the more productive areas. Almost every country increased somewhat the level of government investment in the second adjustment period, in reflection of growing bottlenecks and the increased availability of resources.

Indirectly Productive Expenditure. The civil service wage bill was generally protected from the bulk of the decrease in noninterest expenditure. Chile and Ghana were the only countries that initiated a substantial reform of the civil service. Morocco and Senegal, which had large wage bills at the outset of adjustment, also had large wage bills at the end of the adjustment periods. Wage freezes were a popular policy but generally proved to be unsustainable, sometimes because of the growing unattractiveness of government employment

for skilled employees. Although the rate of increase in employment was typically slowed, declines in the number of civil servants during the adjustment period—which have a better chance than wage freezes of being permanent—were uncommon. There was no clear trend in defense expenditure—a large component of which is wages—except in Chile, Morocco, and Thailand, where it declined.

Commodity subsidies were reduced in the course of the adjustment efforts, and in nearly all countries there appears to have been some sensitivity to protecting the poor during these efforts. Finally, other current expenditure on goods and services took a disproportionately large share of the adjustment in total expenditure; within this category, operations and maintenance expenditure increased in Bangladesh and Ghana and decreased in India, Morocco, and Senegal (the five countries where data were available).

Revenue

The top personal income tax rate was reduced over the adjustment periods, and the number of tax brackets were rationalized. Corporate income tax rates were also reduced; they were unified in some countries (Chile, Morocco, and Thailand), but their structure remained complex in others (Bangladesh, Ghana, and India). Efforts in most countries to widen the personal and corporate tax base and thereby reduce the distortive aspects of the tax were confined to the introduction of a minimum corporate tax and—in Chile, Mexico, and Morocco—to a rollback of tax holidays. Exemptions and preferences in the income tax code generally remained prolific.

Reforms of indirect taxation were more substantial. In particular, Bangladesh, Chile, Morocco, and Thailand all introduced value-added taxes (VATs), but only in the case of Chile was this done early in the adjustment period. Following the substitution of the VAT for

---

ment periods (Figure 8). As emphasized in Section II, a general quantification of the impact of "quality" fiscal adjustment is not feasible.

A qualitative assessment can be made, however, of the components of public sector reform in the eight countries, using the criteria just described. To facilitate this assessment, the group is split into two: the countries that undertook the largest fiscal adjustment (as measured by the decline in their primary deficit), which typically were also the countries that had the highest initial level of expenditure and largest initial primary deficit (Chile, Mexico, and Morocco); and the countries that undertook more moderate adjustments in their primary balance (Bangladesh, Ghana, India, Senegal, and Thailand).

Major Fiscal Adjusters

The structure of the public sector in *Chile* was transformed during the adjustment period. On the expenditure side, capital expenditure was cut severely at the outset of adjustment. But much of this was the result of the replacement of public housing investment programs by housing subsidies (a current expense). The decline was at least partially reversed during the second period to alleviate growing bottlenecks in infrastructure, and capital expenditure on schools and roads increased. Education and health expenditures, for their part, were relatively protected—indeed, spending on primary and secondary education increased at the outset of the adjustment period—and the country's education and health stan-

other forms of sales taxes, receipts (as a share of GDP) from domestic taxes tended to increase. The VATs in Bangladesh, Morocco, and Senegal excluded the retail or at least part of the wholesale sector (or both), while those in Morocco, Senegal, and initially that in Mexico had up to five rates, which made them more distortive, more difficult to administer, and less elastic. In Ghana and Morocco, excise taxes remained important sources of revenue, particularly those on petroleum. There was usually a switch from specific to ad valorem excise rates, which increased their elasticity, but excise tax structure remained complex in Bangladesh, India, Morocco, and Senegal.

The dispersion and maximum rates of import duties declined in all countries—implying some reduction in their complexity and distortive aspects—though the extent and pace of adjustment varied (being most substantial and rapid in Chile, India, Mexico, and Morocco). Export and other international taxes were virtually abolished during the adjustment efforts, except in Ghana.

Administration Efforts

In Chile, India, Mexico, Morocco, and Thailand, the public expenditure management system was comparatively strong in many if not all respects. In Bangladesh, Senegal, and Ghana, public expenditure management was comparatively weak in virtually all respects; of this group, only in Ghana was there some improvement during the adjustment effort. The most substantive improvements were undertaken by countries that had already achieved an effective basic system, characterized by the use of a "top down" approach to establishing expenditure aggregates, a primary role of the Ministry of Finance in the budget process, reliance on tight expenditure control mechanisms during the fiscal year, and the regular compilation of transparent fiscal accounts. Granting the difficulty of assessing the role of public expenditure management in sustaining productive expenditure, it appears that countries with strong public expenditure management systems had more efficient expenditure programs.

More efforts were undertaken to improve tax and customs administration systems than public expenditure management systems. As with public expenditure management, the most substantial reforms were undertaken in Chile, Mexico, and Thailand, which started with a solid basic system at the outset of the adjustment effort, and in Ghana, which, like Mexico, had a high degree of government commitment. Bangladesh and India had great need yet showed little improvement in their tax and customs administration systems, and in Senegal some reform efforts were initiated but were not sustained. The tax and customs administration system was variously compromised in some countries by external factors such as civil service policies, provision of supplies, the tax code, and the revenue-sharing and constitutional arrangements.

Enterprise Reform

Although the data were incomplete, the operating position of the public enterprise sector improved, and the cost of budgetary support declined, during the adjustment period in all countries but Bangladesh. Enterprise reform was typically limited to increases in tariffs during the initial years of the adjustment period; reforms to increase efficiency were generally delayed until the second adjustment period. Reform took a variety of forms including outright privatization, establishment of performance contracts for enterprises remaining in the public domain, and private sector involvement in public enterprise operations. The evidence did not suggest a general rule concerning the relative success of one of these approaches to enterprise reform over another, although all countries undertook at least some steps toward privatization.

dards, which were high to begin with, remained so (Figures 9 and 10). Salaries of teachers and health workers did decline in real terms during the second adjustment period, however.

The pension reform of 1981, which was unique to Chile, stimulated the development of capital markets and reduced labor costs.[35] The gradual elimination of public employment programs in the course of the 1980s, as the country recovered from the severe recession earlier in the decade, contributed to a substantial decrease in transfers and subsidies during the second adjustment period (Figure 5). The public works program offering employment at the minimum wage had a substantial coverage at its peak in the early 1980s, and the evidence suggests that it was well targeted.[36]

Chile was one of only two countries—the other was Ghana—to achieve a substantial restructuring of the civil service. The wage bill was reduced through wage restraint, measures to cut employment, and the

---

[35]Labor costs were reduced to the extent that participants in the new regime saw their contribution—which replaced a payroll tax—as a form of saving, albeit involuntary, rather than as a tax that was unrelated to the future value of the pension. Capital markets were stimulated by the need of the pension funds for domestic financial instruments in which to invest contributions (for a general assessment of the reform, see Diamond and Valdés-Prieto, 1994; for capital market issues, see Holzmann, 1996).

[36]There were, however, some complaints that participants in the program were stigmatized by regular employers (Graham, 1994).

Figure 4. Wages and Salaries Expenditure
(In percent of GDP)[1]

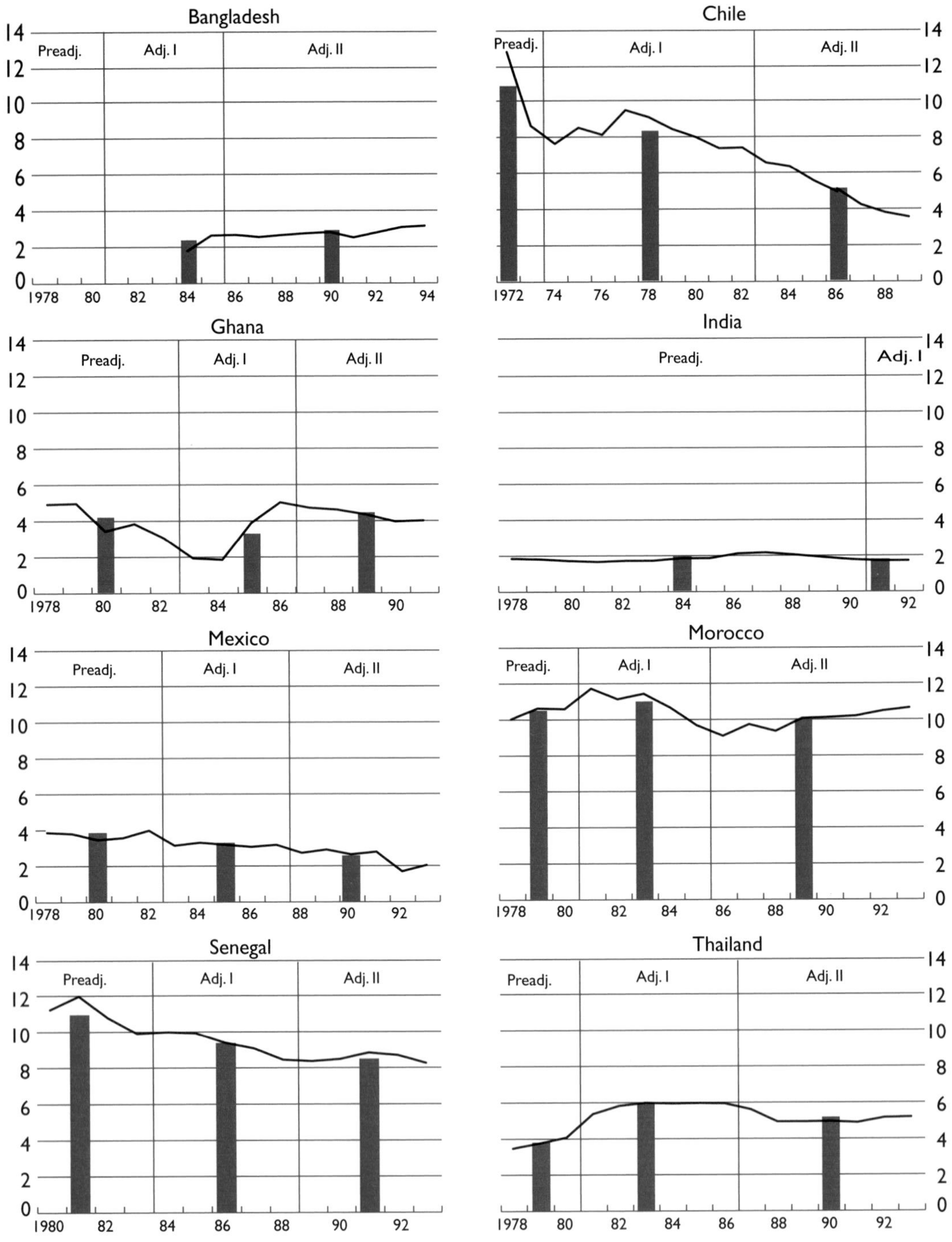

Sources: IMF, *Government Finance Statistics Yearbook* (various years); and various IMF Staff Country Reports.
[1]For Bangladesh, India, and Senegal, data refer to fiscal years. Averages over subperiods are shown as bars.

Table 3. Enterprises and Indicators of Reform
(In percent of GDP, unless otherwise noted)

Country	Preadjustment	Adjustment I	Adjustment II
	Share of value added of public enterprises in nonagricultural GDP		
Bangladesh	3.5[1]	5.0	5.4
Chile	39.0	14.1	12.6
Ghana	7.7[2]	15.2	15.7
India	18.9[3]	...	—
Mexico	14.8	14.5	9.0[4]
Morocco	23.5	17.7	17.8[5]
Senegal	11.1	6.4	...
Thailand	...	6.2	...
	Overall balances of public enterprises before transfers		
Bangladesh	−1.6[1]	−4.1	−1.8[4]
Chile	...	5.8	9.9
Ghana	−3.3	0.9	2.4[5]
India	−2.5[3]	...	—
Mexico	−0.3	3.4	3.1[4]
Morocco	−4.9	−3.9	...
Senegal	−9.0	−1.5	...
Thailand	−4.4	0.5	−1.5[4]
	Privatization initiatives (number of public enterprises)[6]		
Bangladesh	235	—	3
Chile	596	548	18
Ghana	220	—	63
India	236	—	—
Mexico	1,155	538	402
Morocco	620	—	35
Senegal	120	—	47
Thailand	57	—	2

Sources: World Bank (1995a); and various IMF Staff Country Reports.

[1] In 1981.
[2] In 1984.
[3] In 1989.
[4] In 1991.
[5] In 1990.
[6] For preadjustment period, number at outset of the adjustment period; for others, number privatized or liquidated at end of adjustment periods I and II.

devolution of social expenditure to the local authorities, while at the same time salary differentials were widened (see Figure 4). These latter measures began to pay off during the second adjustment period, when the wage bill declined sharply. The transformation in the structure of expenditure just described was facilitated by a public expenditure management system that was functioning well at the outset and was strengthened during the adjustment period.

The Chilean tax system was radically reformed. In particular, the relative efficiency of the tax department made possible the early introduction of a broadly based VAT, which yielded substantial rev-

enue and replaced a cascading sales tax. Similarly, early reform of business income taxation and tax incentives substantially reduced the cost of capital and the dispersion of effective tax rates. The tariff structure was quickly and radically reformed so that the range of effective rates of protection was drastically reduced (Velasco, 1994). The overall reduction in tax collections in the second period—to which the reform of social security arrangements and a reduction in the standard VAT rate contributed—did not reflect any erosion in the statutory base, and compliance remained relatively high. By reducing the average rate of business income taxation and the spread

Figure 5. Subsidies and Current Transfers Expenditure
(In percent of GDP)[1]

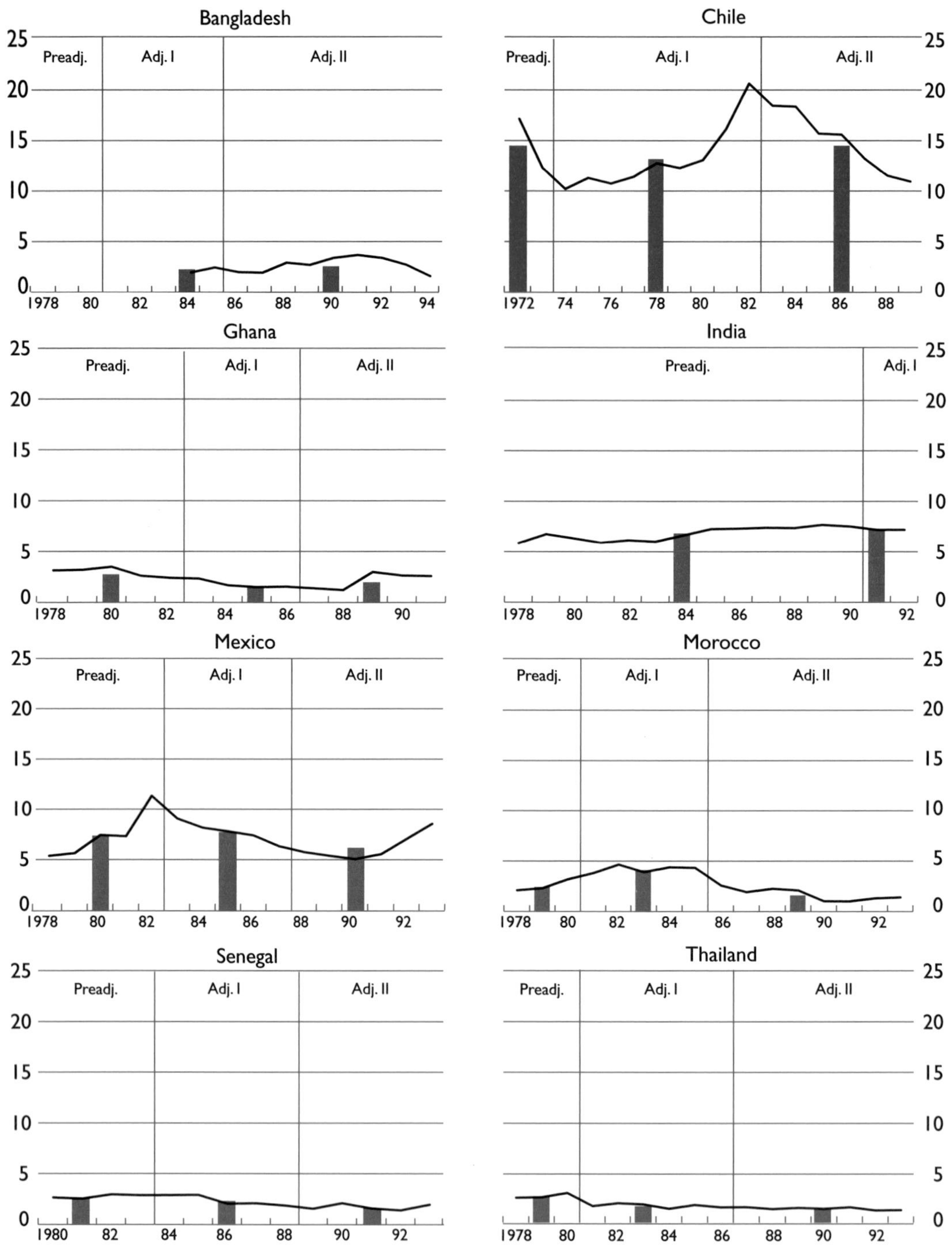

Sources: IMF, *Government Finance Statistics Yearbook* (various years); and various IMF Staff Country Reports.
[1]For Bangladesh, India, and Senegal, data refer to fiscal years. Averages over subperiods are shown as bars.

Figure 6. Other Current Goods and Services Expenditure
(In percent of GDP)[1]

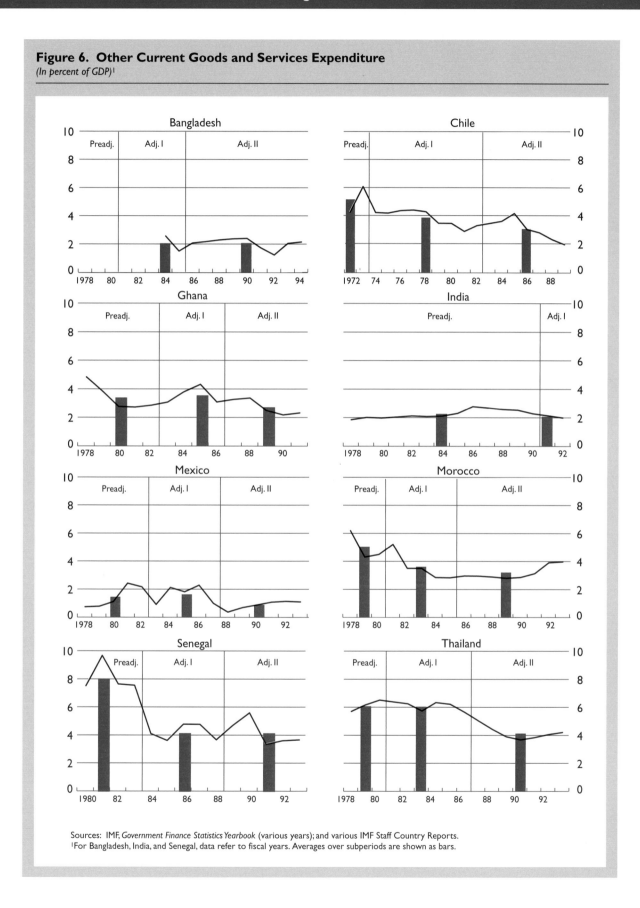

Sources: IMF, *Government Finance Statistics Yearbook* (various years); and various IMF Staff Country Reports.
[1]For Bangladesh, India, and Senegal, data refer to fiscal years. Averages over subperiods are shown as bars.

Figure 7. Capital Expenditure
(In percent of GDP)[1]

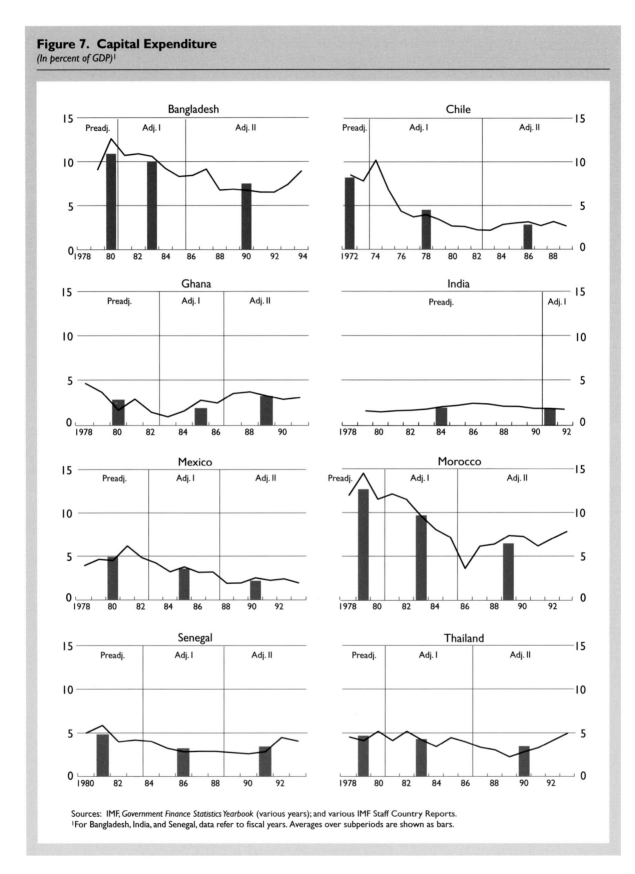

Sources: IMF, *Government Finance Statistics Yearbook* (various years); and various IMF Staff Country Reports.
[1]For Bangladesh, India, and Senegal, data refer to fiscal years. Averages over subperiods are shown as bars.

of marginal effective rates of taxation, and thereby sending a signal to investors that the government was pro-business, these changes, in and of themselves, probably promoted growth. Finally, enterprises were restructured, and the structure of their prices rationalized, as a basic preparatory step for the massive privatization program that began right at the outset of the adjustment period.

The extent of reform in *Mexico* rivaled that in Chile, particularly as regards privatization. With the huge cuts in total expenditure of the federal government, however, Mexico did not maintain the share of primary education expenditure in GDP, even though the share of tertiary education expenditure was increased. But Mexico had already achieved a high level of coverage of the school-age population by the start of the adjustment efforts, and there was no significant change in primary enrollment rates or in pupil-teacher ratios over the period. Similarly, Mexico's health indicators were generally good, but at the end of the adjustment period 11–21 percent of the population still lived an excessive distance from a health center. Capital expenditure declined throughout the adjustment period, and the decline in both public works expenditure and education and health expenditure in the first adjustment period was particularly marked. Subsidies and transfers to enterprises also declined, largely because of the scope of the privatization program, which, unlike the Chilean program, only started in earnest in the second adjustment period. The relatively small reduction in the wage bill was mainly effected by real average wage declines; a bolder attack on excess civil service employment could have been more productive.

The major issue for Mexico was perhaps not what happened to the composition of expenditure, but to its level. Mexico ended its adjustment period with the lowest noninterest expenditure of the group. It is, nonetheless, very difficult to infer that public expenditure was too low. The cuts in capital expenditure might have fallen on projects with a low rate of return. Other current goods and services expenditure declined to only 1 percent of GDP in the first adjustment period, and did not recover. Its level was far below that in other countries, but it had always been low, and the figure might reflect classification errors, since it is essentially a residual. That said, it is quite possible that more revenue adjustment, for a given deficit target, might have permitted an increase in productive expenditure in a number of areas.

The Mexican tax system was sufficiently broadly based, at least in potential, to have made such a strategy possible. The VAT reform arguably reduced the distortions of the old sales tax, although its fairly extensive use of zero-rating and initial reliance on multiple rates both reduced its effective base and in-

Figure 8. Average Real GDP Growth and Average Real Per Capita GDP Growth

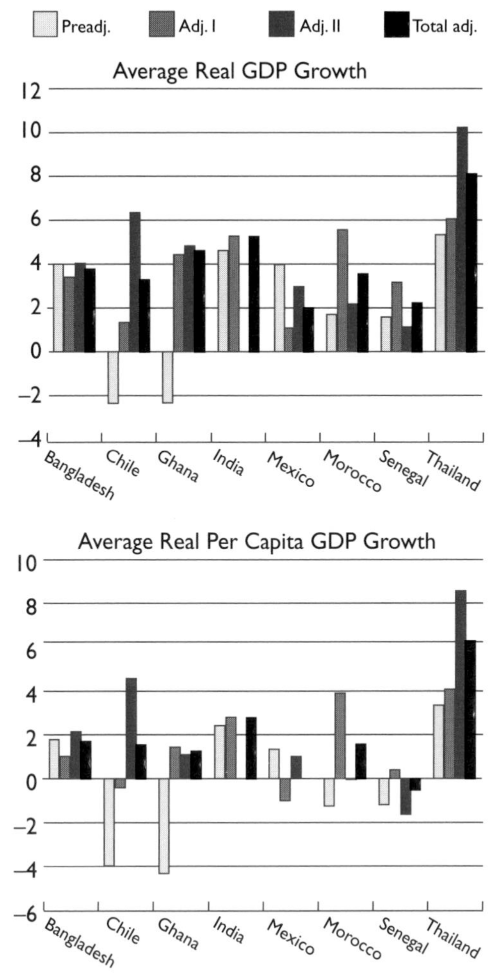

Source: IMF, *International Financial Statistics* (various years).

creased the resources necessary to administer it. Mexico's reform of its corporate income tax during the first adjustment period may have been less substantial than it appeared. It did replace a progressive tax with 11 rates with a unified system, albeit with preferential rates for previously favored sectors. The elimination of the old, progressive system would also have eliminated the artificial incentives to split corporate assets. Because the top rate applied at a relatively low level of income, however, the impact of the reform on corporate structure was not likely to be great. Perhaps more important as a spur to efficient investment was the simplification and reduction in tax holidays and incentives that took place

Figure 9. Indicators of Education Expenditure and Quality

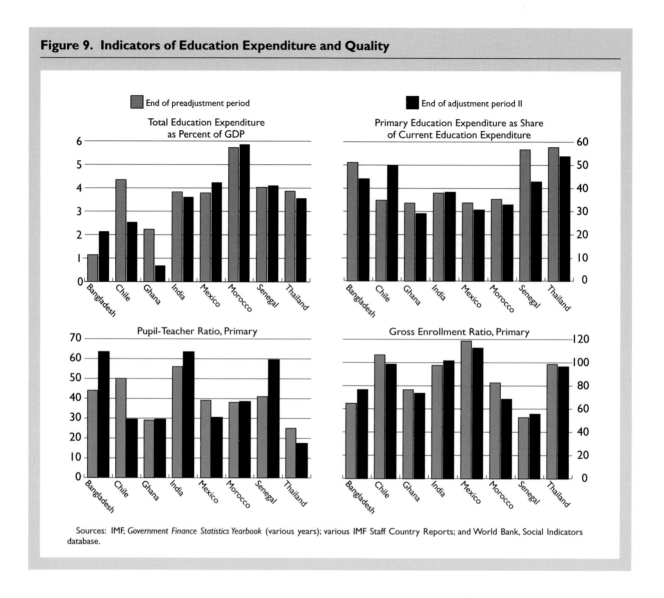

Sources: IMF, *Government Finance Statistics Yearbook* (various years); various IMF Staff Country Reports; and World Bank, Social Indicators database.

later in the adjustment effort. Like Chile, Mexico implemented a comprehensive tariff reform early in its adjustment efforts. Improvements at various stages of the administrative process, in addition to their impact on revenue yield, contributed to a more stable business climate by making tax administration more predictable.

The quality of expenditure adjustment in *Morocco* was uneven. Expenditure on health and education, which was fairly high at the outset of its adjustment efforts, was relatively well protected, albeit skewed toward the tertiary level in the health sector. The share of primary education did not fall appreciably, although enrollment ratios did, contributing to the decline in the pupil-teacher ratio. Civil service employment remained excessive, although average real wages declined. Commodity subsidies were better

targeted, and improved public expenditure management appraisal procedures arguably increased the efficiency of capital expenditure, despite its sharp decline from a very high level at the beginning of the adjustment period.

Like the other countries, Morocco unified its corporate income tax, although its failure to eliminate the temporary exclusion of corporate agricultural income (together with the continued exclusion of agricultural income of individuals from the tax base) distorted the incentive to invest in agricultural rather than nonagricultural activities. The introduction of the VAT in 1986 reduced the cascading effect associated with the sales tax it replaced; however, the prevalence of exemptions, the extensive use of the zero-rate, and the use of multiple rates did not facilitate administration of the VAT. Morocco did imple-

Figure 10. Indicators of Health Expenditure and Quality

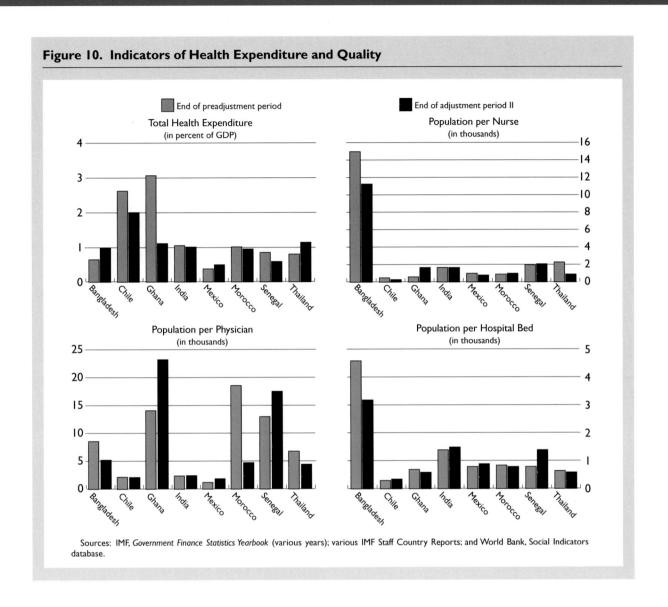

Sources: IMF, *Government Finance Statistics Yearbook* (various years); various IMF Staff Country Reports; and World Bank, Social Indicators database.

ment a major tariff liberalization, although the share of revenue generated by taxes on imports remained high. In addition to tax policy reforms, Morocco also introduced substantial improvements in tax administration toward the end of the second adjustment phase. Public enterprise reform, however, has been very gradual.

Moderate Fiscal Adjusters

Thailand did not start the period with a large public sector or a serious fiscal imbalance, so that a drastic structural change on the order of what was accomplished in Chile was not necessary. Nonetheless, the country's rapid growth allowed it to increase very substantially the level of real resources it devoted to education, and to primary education in

particular. This coincided with efforts to improve the effectiveness of the country's education system and its administrative efficiency. Health expenditure also increased rapidly, with special emphasis on preventive and primary care. As with education, the country's health indicators have now reached high levels.

Thailand's capital expenditure policy is more difficult to evaluate. The decline in the first adjustment period spared the health and education sectors but contributed to the bottlenecks in infrastructure entailed by the country's rapid growth rates. It was subsequently reversed when public expenditure management stopped relying on the rule that capital expenditure in areas other than health and education could only be undertaken once a clear need had been demonstrated for it. The ratio of outlays on other current goods and services to wages and salaries declined, but this resulted at least in part from the increase in the relative price of labor and not from a decline in the ratio of real complementary inputs to labor. Thailand did not have to deal with the problem of a large and inefficient nonfinancial public enterprise sector and was able to reduce subsidies. Finally, along with Morocco, Thailand benefited from a significant decline in military expenditure, albeit from a comparatively high starting point.

Thailand was the only country apart from Ghana where the contribution of revenue to the reduction in the primary deficit outweighed the contribution of expenditure. Because of Thailand's rapid economic growth, most of the increase in revenue came from income taxes, despite the unification of the rate structure and the cut in the average rate of the corporate income tax. The taxation of domestically produced goods and services was reformed in two distinct stages, culminating in the introduction of a VAT late in the adjustment process, whose anticascading features and broad base would have been growth promoting. Thailand's reform of its tariff system was not as fundamental as those of some of the other countries, but its system was less in need of reform to begin with.

In *Bangladesh,* the shortcomings of public expenditure management arguably hobbled efforts to make the expenditure side of the budget more growth-promoting. In particular, the reliance on incremental budgeting and a lack of control over transfers between budgetary heads probably militated against switches in budgetary allocations to more productive uses. Despite very high illiteracy rates, relative spending on primary education actually declined during much of the adjustment period. This trend has only recently been reversed. As regards health expenditure, a greater emphasis was placed on the primary sector, but total spending remained low. The country's investment program—which was largely financed from abroad—remained inefficient, with much of it ending up effectively as operating subsidies to public enterprises. Some trends were arguably growth-promoting, however: subsidies declined in the second adjustment period, in part because of better targeting of commodity subsidies and food-for-work programs, while other current expenditure on goods and services increased from an unsustainably low level.

The failure to increase productive expenditure can in large part be explained by a failure to increase the tax ratio. The tax effort in Bangladesh was the second lowest of the eight countries at the outset of adjustment—a sign of serious problems with tax administration. Bangladesh did, nonetheless, make real efforts to reform the structure of its tax system. This reform included a drop in the top marginal rate of the personal income tax from 60 percent plus a vari-

able surcharge to 25 percent. Given the small number of taxpayers and the problems with the National Board of Revenue, this would not, however, have had a major impact on incentives. The introduction in 1991 of a VAT levied at the manufacturer-importer stage, which eliminated differential rates of sales taxation on certain domestically produced and imported goods, could have eliminated some serious distortions and lowered the cost of capital, as could the moves to rationalize the external tariff. These reforms, however, were not effectively complemented by an improvement in tax administration. Finally, the performance of the public enterprise sector, if anything, deteriorated.

In *Ghana,* expenditure increased almost across the board. This general increase was undoubtedly necessary just to provide a minimum level of public services. In the health sector, however, the share of the tertiary level in expenditure appears to have increased; in education, the share of the tertiary level remained high. Ghana was the one country with serious expenditure management problems that implemented major reforms to its public expenditure management system; the scope of these reforms was enough to make a difference in the functioning of most components of the system. Arguably, these increases would have combined with the lessening of budgetary constraints as revenue increased in the mid-to-late 1980s to boost the rate of return on public investment in human and physical capital. Ghana was able to effect a substantial reduction in the civil service in 1987–90, something none of the other countries apart from Chile achieved. Improved public expenditure management would probably have played a role in this success, although the subsequent acceleration of expenditure indicates the need for a reinforcement of the reform effort.

Much of the revenue to finance these efforts came from the increase in trade taxes following the devaluation of the cedi. Indeed, Ghana reduced the average rate of the corporate income tax without unifying the tax or greatly changing the structure of the base or related incentive schemes. It was the only country to retain a single-stage sales tax, albeit one with an anticascading feature. Ghana's customs tariff had a relatively narrow dispersion at the outset of the adjustment efforts, and this did not change further. The major changes Ghana made to its administrative system, however, clearly contributed to the huge increase—in proportional terms at least—in the yield of its tax system. Substantial reforms were initiated in the public enterprise sector.

In *India,* the bulk of the adjustment effort began in earnest in 1991, so that the time available for fundamental reform has been short. Transfers to the states and subsidies have been reduced—particularly the fertilizer and export subsidies, both of which are highly distortional. Social expenditure has been largely protected during the adjustment, although the need for more expenditure, particularly on health, remains great. Although public expenditure management procedures were generally satisfactory, expenditure control has not typically been effective, as shown by the repeated expenditure overruns of state governments.

The major focus of tax reform efforts was in trade taxes, with a narrowing of the dispersion between tariff rates during the trade liberalization process. In addition, the central excise tax system was strengthened by reducing the number of bands, lowering rates, extending the number of goods under the Modvat system, and use of invoice-based valuation.[37] The recent decision to extend the Modvat's credit feature to capital goods would have reduced the cost of capital. In contrast, the corporate income tax has not been unified, although the average rate was reduced, and tax holidays for new industrial undertakings were restricted but not eliminated. Comparatively little has been done to reform the public enterprise sector.

Finally, *Senegal* was adversely affected during the adjustment period by the corrosive impact on its revenue base of the growing overvaluation of the CFA franc.[38] Because Senegal made few changes to its tax structure and its efforts to improve tax administration were not always sustained, it was all the more necessary to concentrate its fiscal adjustment efforts on the expenditure side of the budget. These efforts were not, however, particularly successful. In particular, the education program appears to have been inefficient in its allocation of resources both across and within subsectors. In particular, primary education's share in the total slipped, and Senegal continued to suffer from low enrollment ratios and high pupil-teacher ratios. Although overall expenditure at the primary level relative to GDP was fairly high, this was attributable in part to the high salary levels for teachers.

Some progress was achieved. In the health sector, primary care was given comparatively more emphasis. The civil service wage bill was reduced but remained high relative to that of other countries. The growing imbalance between wage and salary and other current expenditure, which marked the 1980s, and the poor experience with cost-recovery programs are, however, consistent with the lack of flexibility and incentives for efficiency that characterize public expenditure management in Senegal. Finally,

[37]Modvat is a modified version of the VAT, based on the excise tax system. Only excisable goods are in the tax net.

[38]Much of the tax base would depend on imported goods, whose relative price was reduced with the overvaluation of the CFA franc.

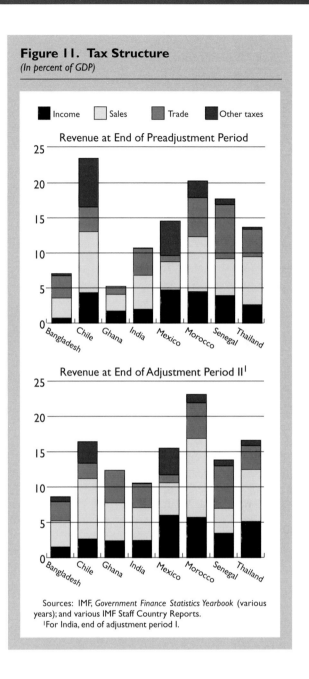

Figure 11. Tax Structure
(In percent of GDP)

Legend: Income, Sales, Trade, Other taxes

Revenue at End of Preadjustment Period

Revenue at End of Adjustment Period II[1]

Sources: IMF, *Government Finance Statistics Yearbook* (various years); and various IMF Staff Country Reports.
[1]For India, end of adjustment period I.

the enterprise reform strategy was at least partly successful.

Where Was Fiscal Reform Most Growth-Promoting?

Among the major fiscal adjusters, there can be little dissent about the proposition that reform in *Chile* was most conducive to growth. Once the financial crisis and ensuing deep recession of the early 1980s had been surmounted, the combination of generally conservative financial policies and retrenchment of the state must have helped to create an environment that fostered growth.

Among the moderate fiscal adjusters, *Thailand* stands out. No major redefinition of the role of the state took place. Instead, sound overall economic policies and a high saving rate, among other factors, contributed to the rapid growth that made possible an increase in social and infrastructural investment, which in turn contributed to growth, thus creating a virtuous circle. Granted the major differences in their starting points and the kinds of reforms they pursued, Chile and Thailand display important similarities. Both countries began their adjustment efforts with the great advantage of well-educated populations; another point in common was adequate public expenditure management. Both made major changes to their tax systems, although the changes to the Chilean system were the more radical; both also implemented administrative reforms. Of interest is that the overall level and composition of tax revenue in the two countries are now similar (Figure 11, on preceding page).[39]

How conducive to growth was fiscal reform among the other major adjusters? In *Mexico*'s case, the overall change in public sector structure rivals what took place in Chile. There is, however, a question about the distribution of adjustment between revenue and expenditure, with the possibility that

---

[39]One significant difference is the lesser importance of general sales taxation in Thailand, a reflection of the comparatively low general rate of its VAT.

cuts in expenditure were excessive. *Morocco* was moderately successful in making its tax system and the composition of its expenditure more conducive to growth; however, it did not resolve overstaffing in the civil service, despite some improvements in public expenditure management.

After Thailand, *Ghana* stands out among the other moderate adjusters, mainly because it increased productive expenditure rapidly, albeit from an abysmally low base; implemented substantial changes to public expenditure management; and improved tax administration. Only Ghana and Chile among the eight countries succeeded in reducing the size of the civil service, although it remains overstaffed in Ghana. *Bangladesh*'s public expenditure management remained unreformed, and, despite certain growth-promoting changes in expenditure composition, its expenditure program remained inefficient. Its efforts at tax reform appear to have been handicapped by a failure to improve an inefficient tax administration. There are parallels in these respects with *India,* where the quality of expenditure does not seem to have changed much thus far during the adjustment period, and public enterprise reform has yet to begin in earnest. Finally, *Senegal* did not reform public expenditure management, and the productivity of its expenditure program does not appear to have improved materially. Despite its quantitative adjustment efforts, it was unable to do much to make its public sector more growth-oriented, except perhaps to reduce the size of the nonfinancial public enterprise sector.

IV Lessons

Lessons from Public Sector Reform

The experience of public sector reform in Chile and Thailand makes clear that, just as a given *quantity* of fiscal adjustment can be achieved in different ways, *high-quality* fiscal adjustment can take quite different forms. It is nonetheless possible to draw some lessons from the Chilean and Thai experiences, and from the experiences of the other six countries. First and most important, stabilization need not play havoc with a growth-promoting fiscal strategy. Even though the imperatives of the adjustment process may require that deep cuts be made in total public expenditure, it is possible to protect most if not all of a core program of the most productive expenditure. Initial cuts can then be at least partially restored once stabilization takes hold and revenue-raising measures take effect.

Second, and as already described, the initial adjustment undertaken by the eight countries tended primarily to emphasize expenditure cuts, particularly expenditure on capital goods and on other current goods and services. Such cuts would have been potentially damaging had they not been reversed subsequently. The increase in revenues and elimination of unproductive expenditure that would make these expenditures affordable, however, would normally require fundamental reforms to tax and expenditure systems. Whatever the pattern of expenditure reduction or tax increases initially adopted, structural reform will, for most countries, be an essential component of sustainable and growth-oriented fiscal adjustment.[40]

Third, the countries that started the adjustment period with an adequate public expenditure management system or made serious efforts to upgrade a deficient system were, on the whole, more successful in preserving expenditure with a high social rate of return. The prevailing pattern of adjustment, with its initial emphasis on expenditure reduction, meant that the public expenditure management system was tested early in the adjustment process. In general, the better the system was able to *set priorities,* and then *enforce the changes* in the composition of expenditure that was consistent with them, the more productive was the ultimate expenditure outcome. A corollary is that some minimum level of public expenditure management expertise is a sine qua non for a radical change in public expenditure priorities and in the efficiency of the public expenditure program. Of course, these administrative abilities can complement, but can not substitute for, a political commitment to a growth-oriented fiscal adjustment strategy. Put another way, good public expenditure management can help to ensure that sectoral targets are achieved, but the establishment of these targets requires a political decision. It is not an automatic result of reforms in public expenditure management.

Fourth, substantial reform of the tax policy regime tended to go hand in hand with administrative reforms; countries implementing substantial reforms to the structure of their tax systems usually had a reasonably well-functioning tax administration to begin with. A poorly functioning administration limited the ability to introduce allocationally superior but administratively demanding taxes such as the VAT, even if it did not prevent some reform measures altogether. A corollary to this point is that the design of tax reform must be sensitive to the limitations of tax administration. For example, a VAT with multiple rates is definitely problematic for a weak tax department. In addition—and as for public expenditure management—there may be a critical minimum level of administrative ability if tax reform is to succeed. Further, administrative reform, when the tax system itself is poorly designed, is unlikely to produce a significant increase in revenue.

Fifth, increases in the tax ratio can be accomplished without major increases in the rates of existing taxes. Conversely, decreases in rates do not inevitably presage a decline in revenue. With the exception of Ghana, the countries achieving substantial increases in the tax ratio did so by broadening the effective base of the tax system, usually with the introduction of a VAT that not only increased rev-

---

[40]This conclusion was also reached in the World Bank's third report on adjustment lending (World Bank, 1992a).

enue but also presented an opportunity to increase the allocative efficiency of the tax regime (see World Bank, 1991b).

Finally, certain structural expenditure reforms that are important or even necessary to the long-run success of the adjustment effort may take time to come to fruition—and may realize only limited budgetary saving in the short run. For example, a civil service reform program that substantially reduces employment may seem unattractive in comparison with a general salary freeze, since it will save little or nothing initially. Yet it is the only lasting solution to overemployment and salary compression. In consequence, such structural reforms have to start early.

Role of Structural Fiscal Reform in Adjustment Programs

This study has argued that maximizing the contribution of the public sector to growth requires attention to the composition of expenditure, as much as to total expenditure, and to the structure of the tax system, as much as to tax yield. Further, the way a tax system is administered is as important as its structure, and public expenditure management systems have a vital bearing on the quality of the realized public expenditure program, translating policy commitments at an aggregate or sectoral level into efficient allocations at the micro level.

The analysis has also emphasized the *importance of appropriate sequencing in expenditure and tax reform* and has advocated that administrative reform must be seen as a necessary component of major growth-oriented reforms of the tax system and the structure of expenditure. One basic lesson for successful growth-oriented fiscal adjustment is that, to the extent possible, it should emphasize administrative reforms right at the outset. The experience of the eight countries suggests that *early reform is more likely to be substantial reform.*

A greater emphasis on administrative reform poses technical challenges for the design of IMF-supported programs. In principle, the experiences described would argue for a greater application of conditionality to administrative reform; however, the scope for this is not likely to expand quickly. Only certain steps in the complex and typically detailed process of administrative reform are readily susceptible to measurement or quantification, given the difficulty of monitoring what has actually taken place. It is also difficult to predict how quickly the various stages of an administrative reform can be accomplished.[41]

This being said, no amount of efficient administration can really rectify a poorly designed tax policy regime or an expenditure program that is inimical to growth. Indeed, the worst outcome would be for a poor tax regime to be well administered. Tax policy measures *can* be monitored, however, and are more readily the object of conditionality.

The study's findings also imply that more attention needs to be paid to the composition of expenditure and to expenditure policy issues, even if national sensitivities make the widespread application of conditionality to expenditure composition impractical.[42] An adequate knowledge of the structure of expenditure, and even comprehensive and timely data on expenditure composition, is often difficult to come by, however.

In view of the intrinsic difficulties in building informed and up-to-date analyses of public expenditure patterns and priorities, especially in the large countries and those with poor databases, the staffs of the World Bank and the IMF have recently strengthened their collaborative arrangements in this area. The objective is to facilitate the sharing of relevant macroeconomic and public finance data and to identify priority issues to be studied in a multiyear work program. Success in these endeavors would mean that advice on expenditure policy would place more weight on preserving the expenditure areas that are critical for growth.

IMF-supported programs are already sensitive to the need to achieve an appropriate balance between expenditure restraint and revenue increases, although the concern has chiefly been with the risk that a lack of balance would threaten sustainability. This study would add to this concern the need to ensure that potentially productive expenditure—such as spending on primary health and education, operations and maintenance, and essential infrastructure—is not cut to the bone. Equally, it is critical to ensure that the composition of spending in potentially productive areas is appropriate (for example, ensuring an adequate balance between wage and nonwage outlays, between new investments and operations and maintenance).

The IMF has for some time encouraged the inclusion of cost-effective and affordable social safety net measures in the programs it supports. Even if they have no direct effect on capital formation and saving, such measures can foster growth by enhancing the political sustainability of an adjustment program. The discussion has also stressed the importance of expenditures on primary health care and education, not only because of their impact on human capital

---

[41]This also makes it risky to assume that administrative reforms can quickly generate additional tax revenue or expenditure economies.

[42]Some recent IMF-supported programs have included structural benchmarks for civil service numbers and the size of the wage bill.

but also because they can have an impact on the income and well-being of the poor.[43] This is an additional reason for supporting a reorientation of expenditure to these subsectors in an IMF-supported program and for ensuring an efficient allocation of resources within them, particularly with respect to the mix of labor and nonlabor inputs.

Finally, it is clear that at times there will be a trade-off between deficit reduction in the short run and certain kinds of structural reform, or effectively between deficit reduction now and deficit reduction in the future. A prime example of this is civil service reform. Employment reduction costs money, and so do efforts to undo wage compression. Clearly, if in any period there is some "maximum" value of the deficit that can be financed, the extra costs of structural reform

will have to be offset by economies elsewhere in the budget. In many if not most cases, countries will be hard pressed not to exceed this maximum value, and in these cases no trade-off is possible. But for budget deficits below this amount, a trade-off may exist. For example, lump-sum severance payments might increase the current-period deficit but will loosen the government's intertemporal budget constraint (by permitting lower levels of expenditure on wages and salaries, hence reducing future deficits). Thus, the study's findings emphasize the importance of viewing the budget constraint not simply in a single period, but in a multiperiod framework.[44]

_____

[43]For more on this point, see van de Walle (1994) and Bidani and Ravallion (1995).

[44]The maximum deficit itself needs to be viewed intertemporally. For example, it may be possible to shift budget financing between periods, raising the maximum deficit in one period by lowering it in another. Assessment of the possibility of intertemporal "deficit smoothing" requires analysis of what level of deficit is sustainable over time.

Appendix I   How Countries Undertook Their Adjustment Efforts

This appendix provides a detailed description of changes in expenditure policy and public expenditure management, tax policy and administration, and of certain aspects of public enterprise reform that took place during adjustment efforts in the eight countries of the study. This material provides the backing for the analysis of public sector reform in Section III. Here the presentation is on an "expenditure-by-expenditure" and "tax-by-tax" basis, rather than the country-by-country basis used for most of the discussion in the main text. The discussion of classification and definitional issues near the beginning of Section III applies to this appendix as well.

Types of Expenditure Reductions Undertaken

Directly Productive Activities

Education

Both *Chile* and *Thailand* began their adjustment efforts with high levels of literacy,[45] high primary enrollment ratios, and low pupil-teacher ratios. Nonetheless, in the first adjustment period Chile increased the shares of total education expenditure and primary current education expenditure in GDP even as total noninterest expenditure was reduced.[46] In Thailand, primary and secondary education expenditure also increased their shares during the first adjustment period, and education policies were reoriented to increase the share of supplies and materials, to upgrade teachers through retraining, and to improve educational planning, administration, and

evaluation. During the second adjustment period, overall public education expenditure declined in both countries as the private sector financed a greater share of education at the higher level.[47]

In contrast, *Bangladesh* and *Senegal* began and ended the adjustment period with the lowest literacy levels of the group, low enrollment levels, and high pupil-teacher ratios. At just 1.3 percent of GDP, Bangladesh was spending less than any other country on education at the outset of the adjustment period. Despite this low share and its obvious need for basic education, Bangladesh was allocating almost one-fourth of total expenditure to tertiary education during the preadjustment period (a high share compared with that in most of the other countries), although externalities in education expenditure are mainly associated with primary education. The share allocated to primary education declined from around 50 percent during the preadjustment period to just below 40 percent a few years into the second adjustment period, when education expenditure was reduced during the initial adjustment effort. The share of primary education did increase, and that of tertiary education declined, when total expenditure increased as a share of GDP toward the end of the second adjustment period.

Senegal was spending 4.0 percent of GDP on education before it began its adjustment efforts. Despite the low average level of Senegalese educational attainment, the tertiary share was relatively protected during the adjustment period. Pupil-teacher ratios at the primary level increased markedly over the period as a whole.

Education expenditure policy in other countries is more difficult to characterize. Although part of the increase in education expenditure in *Ghana* was channeled to primary education, both primary school education expenditure shares and enrollment ratios

---

[45]Literacy levels were around 90 percent in Chile (in 1970) and Thailand (in 1980), compared with levels in 1980 of around 30 percent in Bangladesh, 50 percent in Ghana, 40 percent in India, 80 percent in Mexico, 40 percent in Morocco, and 30 percent in Senegal.

[46]Data on education expenditure by level is available only for current, and not capital, expenditure. Statements about spending by scholastic level should accordingly be taken to refer to current expenditure.

[47]In Thailand, the increase in central government education expenditure during the first adjustment period in part reflects the transfer of responsibilities for primary education from the local to the central government level. In Chile, the decrease in expenditure in the second period in part reflects the devolution of some education expenditure to the local government level.

remained low, and the share of tertiary funding also increased, albeit from a low base. Moreover, in recent years an imbalance between wages and salaries and supplies of necessary teaching materials and infrastructure has emerged (Ghana, 1994). In *Morocco,* education expenditure as a share of GDP declined during the adjustment period, although this was mainly due to declining enrollment ratios (Morrisson, 1991). The decrease in education expenditure in *Mexico* during the first adjustment period led to a severe decline in real education expenditure at the primary level. Real primary expenditure and its relative share in total education recovered during the second adjustment period (World Bank, 1994a). In *India,* the share of total expenditure allocated to the primary sector has not been particularly high, and pupil-teacher ratios are also among the highest of the group.

Health

Judged by standard indicators (infant mortality rates, longevity, and the like), *Chile*'s health status was among the best of the group at the outset of its adjustment efforts. Chile nonetheless appears to have increased the availability of primary care, judging from the decrease in population per nurse. Preventive care remained free; although curative care was means-tested, it remained free for pregnant women and children under six. *Thailand,* with a greater need, was also successful in this regard.[48] The share of its health expenditure allocated to preventive care tripled in the early 1980s as health expenditure was reoriented toward basic care in rural areas, maternal and child care, family planning, and nutritional programs (Wheeler, Raudenbush, and Pasigna, 1989; and World Bank, 1991a). Though average health indicators in *Mexico* are comparatively good, at the end of the adjustment period 11 to 21 percent of the populace were living without access to health care services; moreover, the quality of services and medical supplies deteriorated, especially in rural areas.[49]

The lowest health standards of the group were recorded by *Bangladesh* and *Senegal,* and standards in *Ghana* and *Morocco* were also low, even though at the outset of the adjustment period the level of health expenditure in U.S. dollars per capita in these countries, Bangladesh excepted, was similar to or even above that in Thailand. Bangladesh did reorient expenditure toward primary care, and there were improvements in all health indicators, but total health expenditure remained low, given the country's overall need. During the adjustment in Ghana, the ratio of population per nurse increased, yet that for hospital beds declined, suggesting that the increase in health expenditure that occurred during the adjustment period was allocated more to tertiary than to primary care; access to health facilities in rural areas remained limited (Roe and Schneider, 1992). In Morocco, while cutbacks in capital expenditure affected all levels of health, cuts in operational expenses were focused on hospitals, although health expenditure remains biased toward tertiary and urban health care (World Bank, 1994c). In Senegal, the ratio of expenditure on salaries and wages relative to materials and supplies rose from about 1½ in 1982 to 2½ by 1989; nonetheless, there was also some refocus toward primary care through, for example, an increase in rural health "huts."[50]

Investment

The evidence—which must be treated with some caution because of data deficiencies—suggests that, despite the general decline in capital expenditure, four of the eight countries succeeded in increasing the share of the capital budget allocated to potentially productive areas such as expenditure on education, health, and social infrastructure (for example, water and sewerage).[51] The large decline in *Chile* in part reflected the phasing out of direct public provision of housing in favor of housing subsidies, which decreased capital expenditure and increased subsidies; capital expenditure on roads increased. In *Ghana,* the considerable external project financing available in the adjustment period was used to increase capital spending in priority areas such as transport, agriculture, health, and education, as well as for expenditure operations and maintenance.[52]

---

[48]Given the lack of alternatives, the ratios of population per nurse and per physician were taken as indicators of the emphasis on basic care, while the ratio of population per hospital bed was taken as an indication of the emphasis on more specialized care. The first two indicators are of course imperfect, since both doctors and nurses can be engaged in tertiary care.

[49]Amieva-Huerta (1991). The social security system plays a big role in the provision of health care in Mexico (along with the Ministry of Health). In 1993, the various social security institutes covered about 55 percent of the total population. The private sector covers 37 percent of the effective demand for health care services. The uninsured population is the responsibility of the Ministry of Health.

[50]In Senegal health care is also funded through nongovernmental sources.

[51]For the importance of social infrastructure expenditure, see World Bank (1994b).

[52]It will take a further five years or so to restore Ghana's infrastructure to that available in the early 1970s. See World Bank (1992b).

At the outset of the adjustment period in *Morocco,* the implementation rate and rate of return on government capital investment was low, in part because of the limited capacity of the civil administration to assess and implement project priorities. This situation improved when measures aimed at strengthening project design and implementation were undertaken, and the share of directly productive investment increased. In *Thailand,* capital expenditure on health and education was protected from the overall decline; capital investment in other areas was undertaken only after a clear need had been demonstrated—a restrictive form of expenditure management that was later abandoned.

Nonetheless, in some countries problems that contributed to the initial poor return of capital investment were still evident at the end of the adjustment period. In *Bangladesh,* expenditure declines were concentrated in the transport and communications sectors and to a more limited extent in the health sector; the overall rate of return of capital expenditure remained low owing, among other factors, to complex procedural requirements for project approval and execution and inadequate project evaluation procedures and training of managers, which contributed to a generalized weakness in public expenditure management systems. In *Senegal,* in the initial adjustment period, real capital expenditure declined by over 30 percent, affecting in particular education and to a lesser extent health (Rouis, 1994). Senegal adopted a three-year rolling capital plan in the second adjustment phase with the intention of increasing the overall low rate of return on capital projects. Although some progress has been achieved in project evaluation—more projects are subject to economic and financial appraisal, and staff numbers have been increased—the majority of projects are not rigorously evaluated. The result is that projects with a low or negative rate of return may be approved (World Bank, 1993b). Finally, in *Mexico* the initial reductions reduced real capital expenditure by half, cutting heavily into capital expenditure in health and education (World Bank, 1994a).

In the second adjustment period, Chile and Thailand experienced increasing bottlenecks in roads, transport, and seaports because of their tight capital expenditure policies and rapid economic growth. In consequence, investment expenditure has increased from a low of about 2½ percent of GDP for both countries at the end of the 1980s to about 3 percent in Chile and 4 percent in Thailand by 1993. Similarly, Bangladesh recently increased capital expenditure in the transport and communications, education, and to a lesser extent the health sector, with a decline in capital expenditure on industry, which had in any case effectively functioned as current transfers to cover the operating deficits of public enterprises. Increases were also reported in Morocco and in education and transport and communications infrastructure in Mexico.[53]

Indirectly Productive Activities

Civil Service Wage Bill

Chile experienced the largest reduction in the share of the wage bill in GDP over the course of the adjustment;[54] in *Thailand,* the wage bill increased as a share of GDP despite the overall decline in noninterest expenditure. By the end of the second adjustment period, the civil service wage bill was 8.3 percent of GDP in *Senegal,* and as much as 10.7 percent in *Morocco;* in the other countries it ranged from 2 percent to 6 percent. At the outset of adjustment, the emphasis of countries' efforts to contain the wage bill was on tight wage restraint and not employment reduction. This was the case in *Mexico* during the first adjustment period, when the wage bill declined from 4.1 percent of GDP in 1982 to 3.3 percent in 1988, but civil service employment increased by about 20 percent. Average real civil service wages usually declined, and the differential between the lowest and highest paid civil servants was compressed.[55] As the gap between public and private sector wages widened (to 25 percent in the case of Thailand), the departure of skilled public servants is thought to have compromised the effectiveness of the civil service and often to have required some reversal of the earlier wage restraint.[56]

---

[53]Feltenstein and Ha (1995) found evidence of significant complementarity of public expenditure on communication infrastructure with output in the manufacturing sector in Mexico but, interestingly, not for public expenditure on transportation.

[54]To some extent, this reflected the devolution of education and other functions to the local government, financed by an increase in transfers. However, in all countries, the effective cost of hiring civil servants is often higher than the recorded wage bill because of in-kind payments such as free or subsidized housing.

[55]For example, in India low salaries were increased by 100 percent of cost of living increases, but higher salaries by only 65 percent. In Morocco, real civil service wages declined by 13 percent between 1983–86, yet the lowest wages were increased in line with increases in the cost of living, so that all the adjustment fell on middle- and upper-level wages. In Senegal, real wages for the highest-paid civil servants declined by 40 percent between 1980–90, but wages for civil servants in the middle of the pay ranges declined by 12 percent.

[56]Other factors, such as the power of public service unions, may also have played a role. A large share of defense expenditure is wages and salaries. Only in Bangladesh and Mexico did defense expenditure increase. The largest declines were in countries that started with the highest defense-to-GDP ratios. The direction of change was not always uniform; defense spending increased in Bangladesh, Chile, and Ghana in the first adjustment period, and then it decreased in the second. By the end of the adjustment period, defense expenditure was 2.2 percent of GDP or less in

Only a few countries were successful in permanently restructuring the civil service during the adjustment process. The most substantial reform efforts were undertaken in Chile and *Ghana*. In Chile, salary supplements for skilled civil servants were granted early in the first adjustment phase, the cost of which was offset by eliminating automatic and full indexation of wages with the consumer price index, and by a sharp reduction in employment, except in education and the judiciary (Meller, 1992). In Ghana, the wage differential between the highest- and lowest-paid civil servants was increased—from a multiple of 2½ at the outset of the adjustment effort to a multiple of 10 in 1991—and the number of skilled staff increased. The budgetary impact of these measures was offset by a reduction in staffing at the lower-skilled levels (by 12 percent of the total civil service over 1987–92). These efforts at reform were hampered by a failure to integrate the computerized payroll records of the Ministry of Finance with the records of the Head of the Civil Service.[57] In Morocco, hiring was eventually slowed from an average increase of 6½ percent a year during 1981–83 to 2½ percent during 1984–86, and it remained at around this rate over the rest of the period. However, the continued growth in employment contributed to the high civil service wage bill (World Bank, 1994c). In Senegal, the number of civil servants was held roughly constant by suspending the practice of hiring all university graduates into the civil service and eliminating "ghost" workers. The practice of tenure meant that outright dismissal from the public service was not possible. A voluntary departure program was put in place, but it did not prove successful in reducing overall civil service employment (Rouis, 1994).

Subsidies and Transfers

The cost of consumer good and producer input subsidies decreased in all but one of the countries (*Senegal*) as most prices were increased toward market levels. *Chile*'s efforts were the most substantial.

It liberalized some 3,000 prices at the outset of the adjustment in 1973 and 33 prices of basic foods and public utilities thereafter. In *Mexico*, explicit commodity subsidies declined from 1.3 percent of GDP in 1983 to 0.4 percent of GDP in 1988, reflecting the elimination of general subsidies and their replacement by targeted food assistance programs.[58]

In general, during these price reform efforts, targeting of food toward the very poor was improved by increasing provision of food in exchange for work under the aegis of public works programs (*Bangladesh*, Chile, *Ghana, India, Morocco,* and Senegal) or efforts to avoid increases in the prices of goods that were heavily consumed by the poor (Ghana and Morocco). The most vulnerable groups were also protected during the adjustment period through other poverty alleviation schemes. In Chile and Morocco, distribution of food was better targeted to mothers and pregnant women as well as to children at school.[59]

In Ghana and Mexico, poverty alleviation funds were established (Pamscad in Ghana, and Pronasol or Solidaridad in Mexico) targeting variously the provision of primary education and health, nutrition, water, sewerage, and electricity. Both were established in the second adjustment period. Pronasol concentrated on improving the delivery of basic services and on providing physical infrastructure for the poor, and its total expenditure reached 0.9 percent of GDP in 1993. Like social investment funds in other countries, Pronasol has been criticized for poor targeting and project selection. The sharp increase in transfers in Chile during the initial years of the second adjustment period reflected the cost of public employment programs in the early 1980s and the restructuring of the social security system from a public to a private-based system. Enterprise reform efforts and their effect on the level of transfers from the budget are discussed below.

Other Current Goods and Services—Operations and Maintenance

An evaluation of expenditure on other current goods and services is important for an assessment of the growth-promoting character of expenditure adjustment, both because of its role in maintaining

---

all countries, except India (2.5 percent), Morocco (4.4 percent), and Thailand (2.4 percent)—all countries that either have been involved in conflict or are adjacent to countries that have been involved in conflict. Note that the full amount of defense expenditure is sometimes obscured within other categories in the budget accounts, or omitted entirely (see Happe and Wakeman-Linn, 1994).

[57]The figure of 20 percent includes "ghost" workers dropped from the payrolls. A special fund was established in 1987 to fund severance payments and grants for retraining and relocation of retrenched public employees. At 20 civil servants per 1,000 population, their number is still high relative to neighboring countries, which show figures of less than 10 per 1,000 population. See Leechor (1994) and Nunberg and Nellis (1995).

[58]The tortilla (urban areas) and milk programs (rural and urban areas) relied on geographical targeting (shops were located in poor neighborhoods) and means testing. Mexico also eliminated some major implicit subsidies for the prices of petroleum products, which were hidden in the accounts of the state oil company.

[59]In Chile, social programs were reoriented toward the poorest groups from the outset of the adjustment effort. By the end of its adjustment, half the benefits of these programs flowed to the poorest 30 percent of the population; see Graham (1994) and Meller (1992). For Morocco, see Morrisson (1991).

public sector infrastructure and because the civil service needs some minimum level of complementary inputs to perform its functions. When that level is too low, the efficient performance of even the minimal role that a government should play will be compromised.

Among the eight countries, expenditure on other current goods and services declined from an average of 4.6 percent of GDP to an average of 2.8 percent during the adjustment period. There was an increase in the nonwage component of operations and maintenance expenditure in *Bangladesh* over the adjustment period and in *Ghana* in connection with the rapid increase in priority investment. In contrast, in the initial adjustment effort in *Morocco,* operations and maintenance expenditure was decreased and then held constant in real terms in the second adjustment period; was cut in the adjustment period in *India*; and fell in some critical areas in *Senegal* (see discussion of administrative reform, below).

Tax Reform (Financing Expenditure and Its Distorting Effects)[60]

Shares of Revenue in GDP

On average, receipts from direct taxes as a share of GDP showed little change over the adjustment period, and the bulk of the tax revenue increase was generated from taxes on the domestic sale of goods and services.[61] Collections of the latter, which initially averaged 5.3 percent of GDP and around 35 percent of total tax revenue, increased by 0.8 percent of GDP. This average masks considerable variation within the group; receipts increased sharply in *Ghana* and in *Morocco* (largely because of new petroleum excises) but fell in *Chile* (after the base rate was reduced), *India,* and *Senegal.* In general, receipts increased following the introduction of more broadly based sales taxes, such as the VAT; often, the introduction of a VAT led to a reduced share of revenue from excises (*Bangladesh,* Chile, and *Thailand*).

Receipts from international trade taxes—mostly customs duties—averaged 3.7 percent of GDP and around 25 percent of total tax revenue at the outset of the adjustment period. A fairly constant *average* ratio to GDP over the adjustment periods masks a decline in this ratio in five countries and an increase in the other three (Ghana, *Mexico,* and Thailand).

These divergent experiences variously reflected the lowering of duty rates, exchange rate devaluations, and the easing of import restrictions and foreign exchange availability, which increased the share of imports to GDP.

Effect of the Tax System on Private Sector Incentives

At the outset of the adjustment effort, *personal income taxes* in the eight countries had high rates—top marginal rates ranging from 53 percent to 75 percent—and a narrow base. Reform efforts typically emphasized a substantial reduction (up to 35 percentage points) in the top rate, and in the income level at which the top rate applied (on average a decline from 60 times per capita GDP to 35 times per capita GDP). The minimum taxable income level was also increased in the poorer countries (*Bangladesh, Ghana,* and *Senegal*), which would have facilitated administration. Efforts to widen the base of the personal income tax were more limited. As a result, the personal income tax generally continued to discriminate among different forms of income, and its base continued to suffer from the erosive effects of various exemptions.

As regards the *corporate income tax,* most countries initially had a rate structure with substantial differentiation by sector of activity (as much as 35 percentage points from one firm to another). Certain sectors, such as agriculture, were completely exempt in some countries. Tax holidays for newly incorporated enterprises (implying a complete exemption from the corporate income tax and other taxes for an extended period) were common; this complicated the administration of the corporate income tax. Surcharges and progressive rates were commonly applied (Bangladesh, *India, Mexico,* and *Morocco*), often to compensate for the consequent loss of revenue.

Several reforms were introduced during the adjustment periods. First, in most countries there was a decline in corporate income tax rates of up to 20 percentage points, with the largest declines in *Chile* and Ghana. The rate structure was unified in three countries (Chile, Morocco, and *Thailand*)—countries that also had the best tax administration departments—but remained complex in others (Bangladesh, Ghana, India, and, to a lesser extent, Mexico). Second, there were efforts to broaden the tax base—or to prevent further erosion of the statutory base—but these were essentially limited to the introduction of presumptive taxation or a minimum profits tax (where the receipts could be offset against corporate income tax) levied on gross assets or sales (Mexico and Morocco, which adopted presumptive systems like those already in place in Senegal and Ghana). Some

---

[60]Background data for the material in this section are provided in Appendix III.

[61]Direct tax receipts are defined here as total tax receipts less those from taxes on domestic production, domestic sales, and international trade. Almost all of this revenue would be accounted for by the personal and corporate income taxes.

countries rolled back provision for tax holidays (Chile, Mexico, and Morocco), although preferential exemptions remained prolific in most countries. Finally, inflation adjustment to compensate for the effect of inflation in asset prices on tax liabilities was introduced or refined in Chile and Mexico.

As regards *taxes on the domestic sale of goods and services* preceding the reform efforts, only two countries (Mexico and Senegal) had a VAT; four other countries added VATs during the adjustment period (Ghana was the exception;[62] a modified VAT based on the excise system is used in India[63]). The adoption of the VAT presented an opportunity to reduce the distortive effects that sales and excise taxes can have on the relative prices of consumer goods, since a VAT has the potential to be broadly based without entailing cascading or multiple rates. However, not all of these potential strengths were incorporated in the VATs that were actually adopted.

In particular, while some countries introduced the VAT with just one rate (Bangladesh, Chile, and Thailand), the VAT in Morocco and Senegal had as many as five rates, despite the added administrative complexity this entailed. Further, while the base of the VAT was broader than that of the taxes it replaced, it continued to exclude part or all of the distributive stages in Morocco and Senegal. During the adjustment period, no substantial efforts were taken to widen the VAT base, although Mexico did unify the rate. Agriculture typically remained exempt from sales taxes (Ghana, India, Mexico, Morocco, Senegal, and Thailand). For excise taxes, the major change in structure was usually the replacement of specific rates by ad valorem rates, a measure that would have increased the elasticity of these taxes. In Bangladesh, India, and Morocco, the number of goods subject to excises or the rates applying to them remained high.

For *taxes on international trade,* particularly taxes on imports, there was a general decline in the level and dispersion of tariff rates over the adjustment period, and in the number of goods subject to the maximum rate, as countries shifted from taxes on imports to greater reliance on broader forms of indirect taxation that reduced the excessive levels of protection.

In general, there was a substantial decline in both average nominal and average effective rates of protection, and nontariff barriers were replaced by tariffs. The pace of reform varied, with rapid change in some countries (Chile, India, Mexico, and Morocco) but a more moderate pace in others (Bangladesh, Ghana, Senegal, and Thailand). The slow progress in Bangladesh and Senegal probably reflected difficulties experienced by these countries in raising revenue from other sources, given inadequacies in their tax administration departments. Recently, tariff reform efforts were reversed in Senegal.

Finally, revenue from export and other taxes on international trade—which was low at the outset of the adjustment effort—had been virtually eliminated by the end of the adjustment period, except in Ghana, where export taxes are the principle means by which the income of cocoa growers is taxed.

Public Expenditure Management and Tax Administration Systems

This subsection is concerned with the public expenditure management and tax and customs administration systems in the case studies, focusing on how these systems changed during the adjustment process and on how the systems appear to have affected the implementation and achievement of taxing and spending priorities.

Several qualifications should be made. First, owing to complexity, it is difficult to establish objective criteria for a judgment on whether a public expenditure management or tax and customs administration system is effective and efficient, and hence to gauge the extent to which changes in public expenditure management or tax and customs administration procedures have altered their effectiveness. For the same reason, comparisons of public expenditure management and tax and customs administration procedures between countries—even abstracting from the general lack of data—are to an extent subjective. Nonetheless, even if fine distinctions cannot be made, the differences in the operating procedures are often marked. Consequently, broad conclusions on the likely effectiveness of a change in public expenditure management or tax and customs administration procedures can be drawn, or comparisons of one system with another made, with some assurance. Second, the effectiveness of an administration system depends to a considerable extent on the environment in which it must function. For example, the effectiveness of a system can be reduced if civil service policies underpay skilled civil servants, since a consequence of such a policy may be a shortage of well-trained budget and tax officers. Third, in view of the learning curve, it may take substantial time

---

[62]A VAT was briefly introduced in March 1995, but was immediately withdrawn.

[63]Under the Indian constitution, the central government does not have the power to tax either wholesale and retail trade or agriculture; the taxation of these bases is the prerogative of the state governments. In practice, administrative difficulties have prevented the states from raising substantial revenue from these bases. The Modvat and excise system has recently been revised, with a reduction in the number of bands, reduction in rates, and a shift to ad valorem and an invoice-based valuation system. In addition, the base of the Modvat has been extended to include petroleum products, textiles, and capital goods (World Bank, 1995b).

before changes in administrative systems actually increase effectiveness.

Public Expenditure Management

Budgetary Procedures, Control, and Information Systems

Effectiveness and Discipline of Budget Preparation. Before the adjustment efforts, establishing the annual level for total expenditure by a "top-down" approach—where aggregate expenditure is set on the basis of projected revenue and available financing and then allocated among expenditure needs—rather than a "bottom-up" approach—where aggregate expenditure is set by summing the various expenditure programs that line ministries propose—was undertaken only in *Chile, India, Mexico,* and *Morocco* (Table 4). In these countries, the Ministry of Finance was in charge of the overall budget process, although it naturally acted in consultation with the spending departments to establish budget priorities. Techniques to appraise expenditure priorities within an overall expenditure envelope were not strong in India and Morocco, so that expenditure estimates tended to be based on previous allocations rather than an assessment of current priorities. Early in the adjustment period, *Thailand* also switched to a top-down approach; unlike the other countries, the primary agent in the budget process in Thailand is located in the prime minister's office, and responsibilities for the budget process are shared among a number of institutions that are coordinated through working groups and committees.[64]

In contrast, use of such an expenditure ceiling was not effective in *Bangladesh* and *Ghana*—a difficulty that was compounded by the lack of adequate control of the budget process by the Ministry of Finance. At the outset of the adjustment efforts in Bangladesh, Ghana, and *Senegal,* the level and allocation of expenditure within the budgets of these countries were usually based on the past year's appropriation rather than on the basis of an ongoing examination of priorities, which led to inefficient expenditure allocations and created incentives for expenditure overruns.[65] Further, of these countries only Ghana took steps to

improve this aspect of the public expenditure management system, and then only during the second adjustment period. As one consequence of this approach, development and current expenditure were poorly linked, which compromised the productivity and sustainability of capital expenditure through, for example, inadequate expenditure on operations and maintenance. Indeed, weaknesses in the allocation system were expressed in the lack of supplies and materials provided to the tax administration departments in Ghana and Senegal, which compromised their effectiveness (see below).

Control and Administrative Efficiency. A similar pattern among these countries is evident in the aspects of the public expenditure management system concerning control and management of government expenditure during the fiscal year. The control systems were already strong before the adjustment efforts in *Chile, Mexico, Morocco,* and *Thailand.*[66] New expenditure requests during the year were addressed through the use of a contingency fund in Chile. Strict supplementary appropriation procedures were followed in *India,* but recently these have been used to increase the transfer of resources from the center to the states to cover unexpected increases in state governments' expenditure. Cash and debt management in these countries was on the whole adequate, although the Indian system had difficulty producing timely and consistent information.

In contrast, the control systems at the outset of the adjustment period were weak in *Bangladesh, Ghana,* and *Senegal.* Transfers between expenditure categories throughout the year tended to be made without consideration of expenditure priorities; in Bangladesh, there was also poor control over supplementary spending. Aid- and loan-financed expenditure was poorly coordinated with other budgetary expenditure, which hampered budget execution and cash management. Cash and debt management techniques were not strong. In Ghana, there was some improvement during the adjustment process, as arbitrary cash rationing, which had previously been prevalent, was replaced by a better consideration of expenditure priorities.

Transparency and Timeliness of Budgetary Information. At the outset of the adjustment period, only *Chile, India, Mexico,* and *Morocco* prepared expenditure data on both an economic and a functional basis. *Thailand* joined these countries after

---

[64]This disaggregated approach may have complicated expenditure control. Reductions in expenditure during the year were difficult to achieve, given the lack of flexibility of the public expenditure management system, with the consequence that the actual budget deficit was consistently higher than targeted. This deficiency was addressed by switching to the use of revenue estimates that, if anything, now consistently underestimate total revenue.

[65]Senegal provides a good example of the problems engendered by this approach. The first department to spend its allocation was allocated expenditure from other areas without due consideration of priorities, which created an incentive for departments to spend

their allocations quickly during the fiscal year. This practice also puts the department in a better position to claim a higher level of budget resources in the following year, since next year's allocations will be based on actual expenditure in the current year.

[66]If anything, the control system in Thailand was overly restrictive, with consequent delays in approving release of funds to spending ministries.

initiating its adjustment efforts in the early 1980s, and improvements were also undertaken in *Ghana.* Weaknesses remained in *Bangladesh* and *Senegal,* including classification of some current expenditure as capital expenditure, double counting, and misclassification of items within the current budget, all of which weakened budgetary analysis.[67] Coverage of the budget accounts was in varying degrees partial in all countries. The timeliness of reporting was good in Chile and improved in Ghana, India, and Thailand—where the process is at least partially computerized—but remained poor in Bangladesh and Senegal. In Mexico, the delay in reporting for the federal government remains about 45 days; it is much longer for the states.

Use of a Medium-Term Macroeconomic and Planning Framework

Most countries used a multiyear planning approach to determine part of their budget, although the approach was limited to capital expenditure. The effectiveness of this limited approach depended in part on how well capital expenditure plans were integrated with current expenditure. This integration was most effective in *Chile, India,* and *Mexico.* In Mexico, detailed medium-term projections were prepared as a part of the annual budget exercise, and for the national development plan. In Chile, the coordination between current and capital expenditure planning was improved early in the adjustment period. Lack of progress in other countries (with the notable exception of India) was at least in part a consequence of a lack of sufficiently skilled budget personnel and technical capabilities. In particular, while a medium-term approach was used in *Bangladesh* and *Senegal* for capital expenditure, the approach lacked a strong analytical base, and its coverage was incomplete. In *Ghana,* a medium-term perspective was prepared even before the adjustment efforts had begun but did not become an effective budget tool until late in the adjustment period, once a degree of stability and a high degree of commitment to the system by all units in the government had been achieved.[68] Finally, at one stage *Thailand* had the most advanced medium-term perspective, but the system fell into disuse because of perceived inaccuracies of ministries' expenditure forecasts. The sys-

tem has recently been revitalized, with final expenditure forecasts undertaken directly by the central unit in the budget process.

Advanced Management Procedures

Most of the countries that had comparatively strong initial control mechanisms over expenditure at least partially decentralized financial and accounting management toward spending ministries during the adjustment period. These efforts have not been extensive, since the countries have preferred to maintain a high degree of control at the cost of potential efficiency gains from a greater decentralization. The potential pitfalls of decentralization are illustrated by the experience in *Bangladesh,* where decentralization efforts failed owing to poor overall expenditure control mechanisms. This experience also indicates the necessity of having an acceptable basic system in place before introducing more advanced features.

Tax and Customs Administration

Basic Systems

Many countries made an effort to improve taxpayer compliance and to promote self-assessment during the adjustment process (Table 5). These efforts included improved taxpayer education (*Chile, Ghana, Senegal,* and *Thailand*), the simplification of taxpayer forms (Chile, Ghana, Senegal, and Thailand), and of filing and payment procedures (Chile, *India, Mexico,* Senegal, and Thailand). In contrast, *Bangladesh* did not simplify its forms and procedures, despite their complexity.

Procedures to detect delinquent taxpayers, such as the use of up-to-date taxpayer registers, were not strong in any country except Chile at the outset of the adjustment efforts. Several countries made efforts to improve these systems during the adjustment phase (Ghana, Mexico, Senegal, and Thailand), with Ghana concentrating its efforts on large taxpayers. These efforts were not sustained in Senegal because the computer system was not adequately maintained. In other countries, such as Bangladesh and India, systems to detect nonfilers were weak, and little change was recorded.

Enforcement and collection efforts showed a similar trend. Improvements were initiated during the reform efforts in several countries (Chile, Ghana, Mexico, *Morocco,* and Senegal), including the sending of notices, and the adoption of new penalty structures and arrears strategies. As before, little improvement was noted in Bangladesh and India; in the case of Bangladesh, the routine waiving or reduction of penalties encouraged noncompliance and

---

[67]For example, housing allowances in Senegal are classified under materials and maintenance rather than as wages and salaries.

[68]The experience of Ghana also indicates that early improvements in public expenditure management techniques may achieve little in an environment of financial instability. However, many basic features of the system remained in place and then served as a basis for a more durable reform after financial stabilization had taken hold.

Table 4. Overview of Public Expenditure Management Systems and Recent Improvements

	Bangladesh	Chile	Ghana	India
1. Effectiveness and discipline of budget preparation				
Use of ceilings	No	After 1975, ceiling set by Ministry of Finance (MOF) prior to preparation of ministry spending estimates	Not initially; being established	Yes, but not effectively used
Rigor of approval procedures	Not adequate; complex procedural requirements for project approval	MOF has tight control over process	Little coordination of process by MOF prior to 1986; improved in 1986–90, but further steps needed	MOF strong in approval process but does not rigorously assess ministry requests; states' budget allocations and transfers regularly revised upward during the fiscal year
Effective appraisal techniques	Incremental budget on basis of previous year's outturn	Good	Initially not adequate; improved in 1986–90, with review established in some ministries to improve spending estimates; further steps needed	Usually continuation of past allocative shares
Link between capital and recurrent expenditure	Link between planning commission work and budget not adequate, especially for operations and maintenance expenditure	Fair	Inadequate link prior to reform effort; improved in 1986–90, but need for better link with operations and maintenance expenditure	Division of expenditure on plan and nonplan lines rather than capital and noncapital
2. Control and administrative efficiency				
Control procedures and reallocations of expenditure	Procedures exist but often not followed; increasing use of suspense and imprest accounts, and use of contingency fund for regular operating expenditure	Central control of payment established prior to reform efforts; MOF has strong control and can reassign allocations during year; contingency fund of 8% of expenditure in 1993	Extensive use of cash rationing prior to reform, with transfer between categories without consideration of priorities; improved 1986–90 with procurement and payment procedures tightened; unused appropriations now lapse	Appropriations often adjusted in a discretionary manner; in-field payment and account offices appear to try to increase annual allocations within the region
Use of financial planning and cash management	Not adequate	Well-established system prior to reform; cash management system improved after 1975 with use of single treasury account	Not adequate initially; improved 1986–90, though further improvements needed	No formal cash management process, though daily settlements
Coordination of aid and loans with budget during the fiscal year	Aid management and rest of budget execution and cash requirements not adequately coordinated	Good	Coordination and monitoring of aid with respect to budget improved after 1986, though further reform needed	Fair
Debt-management system	Monitoring of debt obligations of government not adequate	Good	Weak prior to 1986; substantially improved by 1990	Slow, problems reconciling different sources
3. Transparency of budget and accounts				
Classification	Based on line items rather than economic and functional classification; some current expenditure classified under development budget	Very detailed on both an economic and functional basis	Data presented on hybrid economic classification before reform began; improved 1986–90, with reclassification of different types of omnibus categories and preparation of functional classification	Transparency improved after mid-1980s; economic and functional classification

Mexico	Morocco	Senegal	Thailand
1. Effectiveness and discipline of budget preparation			
Yes	Yes	No	Not initially; switch in 1980s to overall ceiling based on conservative revenue estimates
MOF coordinates process and can veto ministries' spending proposals	MOF coordinates process; improved substantially for spending within the capital budget	MOF coordinates process, but does not adequately assess spending proposals; tendency to budget on the basis of past year's outcome; capital spending sometimes approved outside of formal investment program	Tight control exercised, but with many different institutions involved
Spending requests considered in macroeconomic perspective; evaluation of capital spending requests improved with use of cost-benefit analysis	Not adequate	Tendency to budget on basis of previous year's outturn rather than on basis of priorities	Reliance where possible on evaluation of costs and benefits
Good	Fair; improved in second adjustment period	Need for better link	Fair, improving
2. Control and administrative efficiency			
MOF can adjust appropriations during the year in response to revenue shortfalls	Controllers approve commitments on basis of budget appropriations; unused appropriations now lapse	MOF tends to reassign appropriations during the year on basis of which departments run out of money first; spending approval and payment procedures very slow, often bypassed	Tight and detailed, though in consequence slow approval process for release of funds to ministries; rigidities impede expenditure reduction in event of revenue shortfalls
Very effective	Unified account at the treasury	Not adequate	Generally good, though weakness in accommodating off-budget accounts
Unit established to track aid received during the year	Fair	Need for improvement	Fair, improving
Very effective	Good	Improved	Fair
3. Transparency of budget and accounts			
Good	Economic and functional classification of expenditure prepared	Some current expenditure classified under capital budget; double counting of up to 8% of expenditure	Switch in early 1980s from classification on basis of line items, but not transparent; conversion to economic and functional classification possible, however

Table 4 *(concluded)*

	Bangladesh	Chile	Ghana	India
	3. Transparency of budget and accounts (continued)			
Coverage	Overlapping coverage by MOF and planning commission of externally financed projects; some key information is lacking (for example, actual and contingent obligations)	Good, though purchases of military equipment financed off-budget	Reasonably comprehensive; coordination of domestic and foreign exchange budget improved after 1986	Incomplete; use of suspense accounts outside budget
Accountability	Accounting and control failures; breaches often go unsanctioned	Good	Not adequate initially; detailed auditing of fiscal accounts since 1988	More use of internal audit needed
Timeliness, reliability of fiscal reporting	Lack of single authoritative source, hence incomplete and delayed reporting, especially for foreign currency transactions; little use of computer	Good system prior to reform period; computerized	Not adequate prior to 1986; some improvement in timeliness with computerization; further reform needed	Improved, though flow of information to MOF needs to be more timely; computerization of some functions after 1991
	4. Medium-term macroeconomic and planning framework			
Use of macro-economic framework in budget preparation	Judgmental with little analytical basis; development budget prepared on the basis of a rolling three-year plan	Strong coordination of macroeconomic framework and the budget; after 1975 planning authority evaluates and selects investment projects, maintains project databank	Macroeconomic framework prepared but not effective prior to 1986; lack of adequate procedures for approving development projects; improved by 1990, including formulation of capital budget plan	Strong coordination of macroeconomic policy and the budget, though not within a multiyear perspective; high caliber of staff
	5. Management			
Degree of decentralization of financial management authority and responsibility	Decentralization of accounting and expenditure control to spending units in 1980s; appears to have been counterproductive owing to lack of effective controls	Prior to reform, MOF exercised very strong control; same after 1975, but flexibility given to ministries to prepare budgets within an overall ministerial ceiling and to maintain own accounts	Strengthening of capacity of spending ministries needed to increase control over spending	Centralized

the discriminatory treatment of taxpayers. Bangladesh also suffered from the inadequate training of the tax officers assigned to administer the VAT upon its introduction in 1991.

Finally, audit procedures were generally strengthened during the reform period. These changes included computer-aided selection of audit cases (Chile and Mexico), the introduction of an audit plan (Ghana and Thailand), and an office of audit (India). This function remained weak in Bangladesh.

Organization and Techniques

The adjustment period witnessed organizational reforms of some substance. The tax and customs ad-ministration departments had been organized along functional lines (payment, enforcement, audit, and so forth, rather than by type of tax) in *Chile* since the 1960s, and many other countries introduced a similar structure during their adjustment efforts (*Ghana, Morocco, Senegal,* and *Thailand*). This was likely to have assisted in efforts to maintain revenue after the move away from reliance on international taxes to more emphasis on broadly based indirect taxes, a reform that can require a substantial administrative effort in the initial stages. At the end of the second adjustment period, *Mexico* merged the customs and tax administrations as part of a general reform of customs procedures. In *Bangladesh* and *India,* the organizational structure

Mexico	Morocco	Senegal	Thailand
		3. Transparency of budget and accounts (continued)	
Good	Good	Incomplete; some agricultural and capital spending outside budget; efforts made during the adjustment to include the extrabudgetary special and diverse accounts within the budget	Fair; some revolving accounts and externally financed projects are outside budget; improving
Fair	Fair	Not adequate	Good
Good for central government accounts; delayed for state and local government accounts	Fair	Data on project implementation delayed	Good; mostly computerized, with some aspects paper-based
		4. Medium-term macroeconomic and planning framework	
Budget considered in a medium-term perspective; strong coordination of financial policies	Fair; budget prepared jointly by MOF and planning authorities on basis of common macroeconomic framework	Public investment program based on a macroeconomic framework was introduced in 1985–87	Multiyear approach introduced, but fell into disuse due to lack of faith in departments' long-term requests; recently reinitiated using Budget Department forecasts of spending needs
		5. Management	
Centralized	Spending agencies have power to commit and issue payment orders under overall authority of the MOF	Highly centralized	Highly centralized; but some delegation, beginning in the early 1980s, of authority to departments—for example, to transfer limited funds within the same project

was along tax lines, and the level of training of officers was not strong. No substantial reforms were reported.

Computerization of procedures (including computer-aided audit selection) was either introduced or extended in scope during the reform efforts in most countries. It facilitated the cross-checking of returns (Morocco) and helped to strengthen customs procedures (Ghana, Mexico, and Morocco). Noted exceptions are Bangladesh and Senegal, where these efforts foundered because of shortages in the supply of necessary inputs and technical backup to support the computer system. The failure forced a regression to less efficient and slower manual systems.

Measuring Increases in the Effectiveness of Tax and Customs Administration

A good criterion of the effectiveness of the tax administration is the size of the tax gap, although its measurement can be difficult. The *Chilean* tax administration is now among the most efficient of developing countries; the VAT revenue gap (difference between potential and actual VAT revenue) declined from 24 percent in 1981 to 17 percent in 1993, which is within the range of estimates for industrial countries. *Mexico* also reported a significant increase in revenue (by 2 percent of GDP) during its reforms, despite a decrease in tax rates (with a 50 percent increase in the number of taxpayers filing)

Table 5. Overview of Tax Administration and Customs Systems and Recent Improvements

	Bangladesh	Chile	Ghana	India
		1. Basic systems		
Voluntary compliance and self-assessment	Large degree of noncompliance owing to perception by taxpayers of poor enforcement procedures	Taxpayer eduction provided; compliance relatively high (for example, for VAT)	Reform based on enhancing self-assessment, with simplification of procedures and improvement in taxpayer education; lower tax rates improved compliance over the period	Noncompliance estimated to be high
Filing and payment procedures	Complex filing forms and procedures	Tax forms simplified in late 1970s; payment procedures simplified, with filing and payment for most taxes through the banks	Printed taxpayer forms and instructions introduced after 1983	Complex; recently simplified
Detection procedures	Taxpayer identification numbers used only for personal income tax (not VAT); use of multiple rather than single ledger system	Taxpayer identification numbers introduced in 1960s	Accuracy of taxpayer registry improved; focus on large taxpayers	Information systems to detect nonfilers not adequate
Enforcement and collection	Penalties often waived or reduced; staff not well equipped to administer VAT (compared with their ability to administer excise taxes); understaffing of personal income tax work	Strengthened in 1980s through use of audits and ability of tax administration to shut down operations of taxpayers in default; recent reform of customs department	Sending of notices; setting and applying adequate penalties; strengthened customs collection procedures	Protracted and numerous taxpayer disputes partly owing to complex tax code
Audit techniques	Few audits of large taxpayers; computer not used to detect potential audit targets	Enhanced in 1980s; selection of cases supported by computer	Introduced audit plan with requirement to audit largest firms once every three years, and quarterly checks of tax returns of large sales and excise taxpayers	Audit office established
		2. Use of techniques		
Organizational aspects	Direct and indirect taxes administered separately; many local offices with inadequately trained staff; no tax recovery unit established	Functional basis for organizing tax administration introduced in 1960s	Restructured into two agencies organized by function in 1985	Training of personnel not adequate
Computerization	Basic computer system for VAT was to be introduced in early 1990s, but delayed; once introduced, essentially inoperable due to shortage of computer supplies	Extensive and efficient usage of computers	Computerization of tax administration procedures after 1983, including customs	Some use, but scope for further utilization

and an increase in external efficiency (as measured by the time required by taxpayers to file and pay taxes) and internal efficiency (as measured by the time required to process transactions and to detect errors and potential fraud). Estimates of the tax gap in the other six countries were not readily available.

Constraints Facing Tax and Customs Administration

Civil service policies militated against the establishment of sound tax and customs administration systems in *Bangladesh* and *India,* where the tax and

Mexico	Morocco	Senegal	Thailand
1. Basic systems			
Low compliance tackled in 1989/90 with simplification of system to reduce time to undertake a transaction	Self-assessment promoted	Self-assessment promoted, for example, by providing taxpayer education	Self-assessment promoted, for example, by providing taxpayer education
Systems simplified	Customs procedures simplified in early 1990s; quarterly installments introduced in 1993	Tax forms redesigned with provision of instructions; procedures for filing and paying VAT combined and simplified	Preaddressed tax returns mailed; instructions and procedures for filing and paying simplified for most taxes
Improvement in information system, including registries with unique taxpayer account	Need for better identification of taxpayers; tax amnesties in 1984 and 1990 to increase tax net; identification numbers used, but not unique	Before 1986, files not kept up-to-date; 3,500 largest taxpayers included in computerized registry in 1988, but not subsequently kept up-to-date	Use of taxpayer identification numbers and taxpayer master files
Improvement in monitoring and enforcing; new fraud penalties introduced	Procedures for tax assessment, collection strengthened with use of computers to cross-check returns after 1986	System to monitor tax exemptions established in 1989 to reduce abuse, and techniques to address tax arrears established; customs valuation needs to be strengthened	Sending of delinquency notices with referral to audit division for failure to respond
Introduction of computer-supported and targeted audit procedures; requirement that firms be independently audited by certified accountant	Audit function strengthened	Audit function strengthened	Audit plan adopted that concentrated on audits on large taxpayers; difficulty extending audit practices outside Bangkok area
2. Use of techniques			
Tax administration restructured; responsibility for collection of VAT removed from states to increase efficiency of administration	Tax administration reorganized along functional lines from mid-1991; increased coordination between regional tax centers established after 1991	Before 1986, tax administration organized along tax lines; structure streamlined in 1987 based on functional approach; new regional tax offices opened	Tax administration restructured in 1983 along functional lines
Computer systems development privatized; all local tax offices and customs houses computerized; possibility for fraud decreased with computerization	More extensive use of computers—for example, in VAT administration and in pilot customs area at Casablanca; supplies increased to tax and customs administration in order to improve efficiency	Computerization used to detect late payers and nonfilers; customs procedures computerized, but some problems experienced with maintenance of system	Computerization of system being phased in, beginning with Bangkok area

customs administration departments do not have the authority to select, reallocate, or discipline their own officers. In *Ghana,* the system was improved with the removal of the tax and customs administration department from the civil service, which enabled the employment of skilled personnel with adequate salaries, improved flexibility in hiring and firing, and facilitated in the purchase of necessary physical equipment.

As described above, several governments changed parts of the tax code in part to alleviate administrative difficulties and reduce evasion (Ghana, *Mexico,*

Morocco, and *Senegal*)—for example, through the introduction of minimum corporate taxes. As noted above, however, tax systems often remained overly complex, in large measure because of the prevalence of tax holidays and other privileges. The complexity of the tax codes in *Bangladesh* and *India* contributed to the problems of these countries' tax departments.

An important source of tax and customs administration difficulties in some countries was the relationship between the central and local government with respect to the assignment of revenue responsibilities and revenue-sharing arrangements. In India, the constitution gives the right to tax retail and wholesale trade to the state governments rather than to the central government. In practice, this has prevented the introduction of a modern national VAT system, while weaknesses in the tax administrative capacities of the states have prevented the collection of revenue from retail and wholesale trade.

Revenue-sharing arrangements have also been an important factor in shaping the tax structure, hence the efficiency, with which the tax system is administered. In India, the central government has tended to rely on international trade taxes as well as the complex excise system, since revenue from these taxes is not shared with the states, despite the distorting effects this excessive reliance entails.[69] In Mexico, revenue-sharing arrangements have compromised the ability of the tax administration to collect VAT obligations. State governments were originally allocated a share of total VAT receipts that bore no relation to the share actually collected from their state, so that they had little incentive to make a vigorous collection effort. To alleviate this problem, after 1987 the states were allowed to keep 35 percent of the receipts they collected over a certain threshold. In 1992, the federal government assumed responsibility for collecting the VAT. In Morocco, the central government allocates 30 percent of VAT receipts to the local governments, with their respective shares determined by population size. A more complex formula, based on tax effort among other things, was envisaged during the last years of the adjustment effort, with a view to increasing exploitation of the local tax base.

Public Enterprises

Countries took different approaches to increasing the efficiency of their public enterprise sectors during the adjustment period, and again the intensity of their reform efforts varied. The most ambitious privatization efforts were followed in *Chile* and *Mexico,* which had among the largest programs in the world.[70] In both countries, the vast majority of public enterprises had been transferred to the private sector by the end of the adjustment period, with the considerable receipts raised (averaging 1 percent of GDP a year in Chile and Mexico during the main years of the privatization program) used to fund social and capital public expenditure (in the case of Chile) or to reduce public debt (in the case of Mexico). The rate of return for the enterprises that had been privatized often increased substantially (Hachette and Lüders, 1993; and examples in Galal and Shirley, 1994).

The experience with privatization in other countries was less successful. In *Bangladesh,* the public enterprise sector was inefficient and a significant drain on the budget, which constrained the availability of budgetary resources for more productive expenditure. Privatization efforts of small enterprises began in the 1980s, though many later went bankrupt. Efforts began again in 1991 but have been slow because of the poor financial state of enterprises and difficulties in establishing an appropriate institutional arrangement for the transfer of ownership. After a slow start, privatization efforts have been more successful in *Senegal.* As in other countries, enterprises were inefficient at the outset of the adjustment period; in 1982, output per worker was 70 percent of the average for all enterprises in the modern sector, yet wages were 20 percent higher than the average (Rouis, 1994). Liquidation and privatization procedures affecting around half of the enterprises began in earnest during the second adjustment period, and one-third of the remaining enterprises have been placed under performance contracts; direct budgetary subsidies declined.

Several other countries have instead focused—at least initially—on achieving enterprise reform through the establishment of performance contracts rather than through privatization. During the second adjustment period in *Ghana,* annual performance agreements with respect to cost and profitability and liberalization of the administrative environment were established in order to phase out budgetary support. A government commission was established to monitor the fulfillment of these contracts and to recommend liquidation where appropriate; around one-fourth of enterprises had been either liquidated or privatized by 1991, and operating profits had improved.

In *Morocco,* reform efforts were made to improve the performance, monitoring, and control of public enterprises in the early 1980s, but these were gener-

---

[69]The recent reductions in customs duties in India are an aspect behind the current review of revenue-sharing arrangements.

[70]In Mexico, of some 1,155 public enterprises in 1982, over 900 had been divested by 1992.

ally ad hoc and met with only limited success. A more comprehensive program was followed in the second adjustment period, which included changes in tariffs and pricing policies; strengthening of the planning, execution, and monitoring of enterprise investment; restructuring of the government's role from one of controlling the day-to-day operations of public enterprises to one of establishing performance objectives; opening of some sectors traditionally dominated by public enterprises to private competition; and, finally, taking privatization initiatives. As a result, total current and capital transfers from the government to public enterprises have declined. A reform strategy for public enterprises in *India* has been initiated; its major elements are increased autonomy and accountability, and the sale of substantial minority shares in a number of units to the private sector. Little overall improvement in performance has yet been registered.

Finally, *Thailand*'s privatization program in the first half of the 1980s was limited to small and medium-sized enterprises, owing to political opposition to privatization efforts for large enterprise. A major effort at privatization was not necessary, because the nonfinancial public enterprise sector was not particularly large to begin with. After the mid-1980s, the private sector was invited to participate in the operations of large-scale enterprises through partial equity sales, joint ventures, leasing, contracting, and franchising. By the end of the 1980s, the combined financial balance of enterprises was near balance, reflecting increased prices and tariffs and reduced operating costs, and most budget subsidies to enterprises had been eliminated.

Appendix II   Expenditure and Tax Categories

Appendix II presents background information (referred to in the text) on selected economic and functional categories of expenditure, and major tax categories, expressed as a percentage of GDP (Tables 6–11).

Table 6. Selected Functional Categories of Expenditure
(In percentage points of GDP)

Country	Level		Change			Share in Total Expenditure	
	Initial	End of period	Overall	Adj. I	Adj. II	Initial	End of period
Education							
Bangladesh	1.3	2.2	0.9	0.2	0.7	6.9	13.5
Chile	4.4	2.6	−1.8	0.7	−2.5	12.5	13.3
Ghana	2.2	3.1	0.8	1.1	−0.3	23.0	18.7
India[1]	3.8	3.6	−0.2	−0.2	...	...	...
Mexico	3.8	4.0	0.1	−1.2	1.3	17.1	28.9
Morocco	5.7	5.9	0.1	−0.7	0.8	19.2	24.6
Senegal[2]	4.0	4.1	0.1	−0.5	0.5	16.4	22.9
Thailand	3.9	3.6	−0.3	—	−0.3	20.7	22.8
Average	3.7	3.6	—	−0.1	—	16.6	20.7
Health							
Bangladesh	0.6	1.0	0.4	—	0.4	3.1	6.2
Chile	2.6	2.0	−0.6	−0.3	−0.3	7.5	10.4
Ghana	0.7	1.1	0.4	0.5	—	7.1	6.8
India[1]	1.1	1.0	—	—	...	...	...
Mexico	0.4	0.4	—	—	—	1.7	2.9
Morocco	1.0	1.0	−0.1	−0.1	0.1	3.4	4.0
Senegal[2]	0.9	0.6	−0.3	−0.2	−0.1	3.5	3.3
Thailand	0.8	1.1	0.3	0.4	−0.1	4.3	7.3
Average	1.0	1.0	—	—	—	4.4	5.8
Defense							
Bangladesh	1.2	1.5	0.3	—	0.3	6.2	9.2
Chile	3.5	2.2	−1.3	0.4	−1.7	10.0	11.5
Ghana	0.7	0.6	−0.2	0.2	−0.3	7.6	3.6
India	2.9	2.5	−0.4	−0.4	...	15.9	15.5
Mexico	0.5	0.6	0.1	0.1	0.1	2.1	4.4
Morocco	5.9	4.4	−1.5	−1.2	−0.3	19.9	18.6
Senegal	2.5	2.1	−0.5	−0.4	—	10.2	11.4
Thailand	4.2	2.4	−1.8	−0.5	−1.3	22.6	15.6
Average	2.7	2.0	−0.6	−0.2	−0.5	11.8	11.2

Sources: IMF, *Government Finance Statistics Yearbook* (various issues); and various IMF Staff Country Reports.
[1]General government.
[2]Current spending only.

Table 7. Selected Economic Categories of Expenditure
(In percentage points of GDP)

Country	Level		Change			Share in Total Expenditure	
	Initial	End of period	Overall	Adj. I	Adj. II	Initial	End of period
Wages and salaries							
Bangladesh	...	3.2	...	...	0.5	...	20.4
Chile	8.7	3.6	−5.1	−1.2	−3.9	25.0	19.0
Ghana	3.2	4.1	0.9	2.0	−1.0	32.4	25.1
India	1.9	1.8	−0.1	−0.1	...	10.3	11.3
Mexico	4.1	2.1	−2.0	−0.8	−1.2	18.3	15.5
Morocco	10.7	10.7	—	−0.9	0.9	35.8	44.9
Senegal	10.0	8.3	−1.7	−1.5	−0.2	40.7	46.4
Thailand	4.2	5.3	1.1	1.9	−0.8	22.2	33.7
Average (excluding Bangladesh)	6.1	5.1	−1.0	−0.1	−1.0	26.4	28.0
Other current goods and services							
Bangladesh	...	2.2	...	...	0.7	...	13.7
Chile	6.1	2.0	−4.1	−2.8	−1.3	17.5	10.3
Ghana	2.9	2.4	−0.5	0.2	−0.8	29.7	14.4
India	2.3	2.0	−0.3	−0.3	...	12.8	12.7
Mexico	2.2	1.1	−1.1	−1.2	0.1	9.8	8.3
Morocco	4.5	4.0	−0.5	−1.7	1.1	15.1	16.8
Senegal	7.6	3.7	−3.9	−3.9	—	30.9	20.5
Thailand	6.5	4.2	−2.3	−0.9	−1.4	34.8	27.1
Average (excluding Bangladesh)	4.6	2.8	−1.8	−1.5	−0.4	21.5	15.7
Subsidies and transfers							
Bangladesh	...	1.5	...	...	−0.8	...	9.4
Chile	12.2	10.9	−1.4	8.3	−9.7	35.0	56.7
Ghana	2.3	2.5	0.2	−0.9	1.1	23.6	15.2
India	7.4	7.1	−0.3	−0.3	...	41.2	44.6
Mexico[1]	11.2	8.5	−2.8	−5.0	2.2	50.1	61.9
Morocco	3.1	1.3	−1.8	1.1	−2.9	10.4	5.5
Senegal	2.8	1.9	−0.9	−1.0	0.1	9.2	7.8
Thailand	2.8	1.1	−1.7	−1.4	−0.3	14.9	7.2
Average (excluding Bangladesh)	6.0	4.7	−1.2	0.1	−1.6	26.4	28.4
Capital							
Bangladesh	12.6	9.0	−3.7	−4.3	0.6	67.2	56.4
Chile[2]	7.9	2.7	−5.2	−5.6	0.5	22.5	14.0
Ghana	1.4	7.4	6.0	5.9	0.1	14.3	45.3
India	1.9	1.8	−0.1	−0.1	...	10.8	11.6
Mexico	4.9	2.0	−2.9	−1.7	−1.3	21.8	14.3
Morocco	11.6	7.8	−3.7	−4.4	0.7	38.7	32.8
Senegal	4.2	4.1	−0.1	−1.3	1.2	17.1	22.8
Thailand	5.2	5.0	−0.3	−1.2	1.0	27.9	31.9
Average	6.2	5.0	−1.2	−1.6	0.4	27.5	28.6

Sources: IMF, *Government Finance Statistics Yearbook* (various issues); and various IMF Staff Country Reports.

[1]Includes exchange rate subsidies between 1982 and 1987.

[2]Excludes net lending, which in 1973, 1982, and 1989 equaled 0.9, −2.9, and −0.9 percent of GDP, respectively.

Table 8. Categories of Revenue[1]
(In percentage points of GDP)

Country	Level		Change			Share in Total Revenue	
	Initial	End of period	Overall	Adj. I	Adj. II	Initial	End of period
Tax revenue							
Bangladesh	7.1	8.7	1.6	−0.2	1.8	81.9	76.9
Chile	23.5	16.5	−7.1	−0.5	−6.6	81.8	77.0
Ghana	5.3	12.4	7.2	6.9	0.3	87.1	90.2
India	10.8	10.6	−0.2	−0.2	...	79.6	74.3
Mexico	14.6	15.5	0.9	1.4	−0.4	93.0	91.4
Morocco	20.3	23.2	2.8	−2.0	4.9	92.0	86.3
Senegal	17.8	13.9	−3.9	−3.4	−0.5	93.6	86.1
Thailand	13.7	16.7	3.0	0.2	2.8	91.9	90.1
Average	14.1	14.7	0.5	0.3	0.3	87.6	84.0
Direct taxes							
Bangladesh	1.0	2.3	1.2	0.3	0.9	12.2	20.0
Chile	11.3	5.8	−5.6	−2.0	−3.6	39.4	26.9
Ghana	1.7	2.4	0.7	0.9	−0.3	28.8	17.6
India	2.1	2.6	0.5	0.5	...	15.2	18.0
Mexico	9.7	9.9	0.2	−0.2	0.4	61.8	57.9
Morocco	6.9	7.0	—	−1.5	1.5	31.4	25.9
Senegal	4.8	4.5	−0.3	−0.4	0.1	25.3	27.7
Thailand	2.9	5.9	3.0	0.6	2.4	19.7	32.1
Average	5.1	5.0	—	−0.2	0.2	29.2	28.3
Indirect taxes							
Bangladesh	6.0	6.4	0.4	−0.5	0.9	69.7	56.9
Chile	12.2	10.7	−1.5	1.6	−3.0	42.4	50.1
Ghana	3.5	10.0	6.5	5.9	0.6	58.3	72.6
India	8.7	8.0	−0.7	−0.7	...	64.3	56.3
Mexico	4.9	5.7	0.8	1.6	−0.8	31.3	33.5
Morocco	13.4	16.2	2.8	−0.6	3.4	60.7	60.4
Senegal	13.0	9.4	−3.5	−3.0	−0.5	68.3	58.4
Thailand	10.8	10.7	—	−0.4	0.4	72.2	58.0
Average	9.1	9.6	0.6	0.5	0.1	58.4	55.8
Nontax revenue							
Bangladesh	1.6	2.6	1.0	0.1	0.9	18.1	23.1
Chile	5.2	4.9	−0.3	1.2	−1.5	18.2	23.0
Ghana	0.8	1.4	0.6	0.8	−0.2	12.9	9.8
India	2.8	3.7	0.9	0.9	...	20.4	25.7
Mexico	1.1	1.5	0.4	—	0.4	7.0	8.6
Morocco	1.8	3.7	1.9	0.6	1.3	8.0	13.7
Senegal	1.2	2.2	1.0	2.0	−1.0	6.4	13.9
Thailand	1.2	1.8	0.6	0.4	0.2	8.1	9.9
Average	2.0	2.7	0.8	0.7	—	12.4	16.0

Sources: IMF, *Government Finance Statistics Yearbook* (various issues); and various IMF Staff Country Reports.
[1] Excluding grants.

Table 9. Direct Taxes
(In percentage points of GDP)

Country	Level		Change			Share in Total Revenue	
	Initial	End of period	Overall	Adj. I	Adj. II	Initial	End of period
Income taxes							
Bangladesh	0.8	1.5	0.8	0.2	0.6	8.7	13.7
Chile	4.4	2.7	−1.7	1.3	−3.0	15.2	12.6
Ghana	1.7	2.4	0.7	0.9	−0.2	28.6	17.7
India	2.0	2.5	0.5	0.5	...	14.8	17.4
Mexico[1]	4.8	6.0	1.3	−0.8	2.1	30.4	35.5
Morocco	4.5	5.7	1.2	0.1	1.2	20.4	21.4
Senegal	4.0	3.5	−0.5	−0.4	−0.1	20.9	21.6
Thailand	2.7	5.2	2.5	0.5	2.0	17.8	28.0
Average	3.1	3.7	0.6	0.3	0.4	19.6	21.0
Personal income taxes							
Bangladesh	0.2	0.4	0.2	—	0.1	2.8	3.5
Chile[2]	2.6	0.9	−1.7	0.9	−2.6	9.1	4.4
Ghana	0.9	0.7	−0.1	0.2	−0.3	14.4	5.3
India	1.0	1.1	0.1	0.1	...	7.4	7.9
Mexico[3]	2.6	2.6	0.1	−0.7	0.7	16.3	15.5
Morocco	1.5	2.8	1.3	0.4	0.9	6.7	10.4
Senegal	2.6	2.5	−0.1	−0.3	0.1	13.7	15.4
Thailand	1.1	1.8	0.6	0.6	—	7.6	9.5
Average	1.6	1.6	—	0.2	−0.1	9.7	9.0
Corporate and other income taxes							
Bangladesh	0.5	1.2	0.6	0.2	0.5	5.9	10.2
Chile[2]	1.7	1.8	—	0.4	−0.4	6.0	8.2
Ghana	0.9	1.7	0.8	0.8	0.1	14.2	12.4
India	1.0	1.4	0.4	0.4	...	7.4	9.6
Mexico[3]	2.2	3.4	1.2	−0.1	1.3	14.1	20.0
Morocco	3.0	2.9	−0.1	−0.3	0.2	13.8	11.0
Senegal	1.4	1.0	−0.4	−0.1	−0.2	7.2	6.3
Thailand	1.5	3.4	1.9	−0.1	2.0	10.2	18.4
Average	1.5	2.1	0.6	0.1	0.5	9.9	12.0
Other direct taxes							
Bangladesh	0.3	0.7	0.4	0.1	0.3	3.5	6.3
Chile	7.0	3.1	−3.9	−3.3	−0.6	24.2	14.4
Ghana	—	—	—	—	—	0.2	−0.1
India	0.1	0.1	—	—	...	0.4	0.6
Mexico[4]	4.9	3.8	−1.1	0.6	−1.7	31.4	22.4
Morocco	2.4	1.2	−1.2	−1.5	0.3	11.0	4.5
Senegal	0.8	1.0	0.1	—	0.2	4.4	6.0
Thailand	0.3	0.8	0.5	—	0.4	1.9	4.1
Average	2.0	1.3	−0.7	−0.5	−0.1	9.6	7.3

Sources: IMF, *Government Finance Statistics Yearbook* (various issues); and various IMF Staff Country Reports.

[1]Excludes corporate taxes paid by PEMEX.

[2]Allocation of income taxes in final period based on shares in 1986 receipts.

[3]Allocation of income taxes in final period based on shares in 1988 receipts.

[4]Includes income taxes from PEMEX.

Table 10. Taxes on Domestic Sales of Goods and Services
(In percentage points of GDP)

Country	Level		Change			Share in Total Revenue	
	Initial	End of period	Overall	Adj. I	Adj. II	Initial	End of period
			Total				
Bangladesh	2.9	3.7	0.9	−0.1	1.0	33.1	33.1
Chile	8.7	8.5	−0.2	4.0	−4.2	30.3	39.9
Ghana	2.4	5.4	3.0	1.5	1.5	39.2	39.0
India	4.8	4.6	−0.2	−0.2	...	35.8	32.6
Mexico	4.0	4.6	0.6	1.7	−1.2	25.7	26.9
Morocco	7.8	11.2	3.3	0.5	2.8	35.5	41.6
Senegal	5.3	3.4	−1.9	−1.1	−0.7	27.8	21.1
Thailand	6.9	7.4	0.5	0.6	−0.1	46.0	39.8
Average	5.3	6.1	0.8	0.9	−0.1	34.2	34.2
			Sales and value-added taxes				
Bangladesh	1.4	2.5	1.0	−0.4	1.4	16.5	21.8
Chile	5.2	6.8	1.6	5.4	−3.9	18.2	31.7
Ghana	0.2	1.2	0.9	0.4	0.5	4.0	8.4
India	0.1	0.2	—	—	...	1.0	1.1
Mexico	2.2	2.9	0.7	1.0	−0.3	14.2	17.0
Morocco	5.0	5.9	0.9	1.0	−0.1	22.4	21.8
Senegal	3.6	3.0	−0.6	−0.2	−0.4	18.7	18.3
Thailand	2.8	3.0	0.3	−0.2	0.5	18.4	16.3
Average	2.6	3.2	0.6	0.9	−0.3	14.2	17.0
			Excises and other goods and services taxes				
Bangladesh	1.4	1.3	−0.1	0.2	−0.4	16.6	11.4
Chile	3.5	1.8	−1.7	−1.5	−0.3	12.1	8.2
Ghana	2.1	4.2	2.1	1.1	1.0	35.3	30.6
India	4.7	4.5	−0.2	−0.2	...	34.7	31.5
Mexico	1.8	1.7	−0.1	0.7	−0.8	11.5	9.9
Morocco	2.9	5.3	2.4	−0.5	2.9	13.1	19.8
Senegal	1.7	0.6	−1.2	−1.0	−0.2	9.1	3.5
Thailand	4.1	4.3	0.2	0.8	−0.6	27.6	23.5
Average	2.8	3.0	0.2	—	0.2	20.0	17.3

Sources: IMF, *Government Finance Statistics Yearbook* (various issues); and various IMF Staff Country Reports.

Table 11. Taxes on External Trade
(In percentage points of GDP)

Country	Level		Change			Share in Total Revenue	
	Initial	End of period	Overall	Adj. I	Adj. II	Initial	End of period
			Total				
Bangladesh	3.2	2.7	−0.5	−0.3	−0.1	36.7	23.8
Chile	3.5	2.2	−1.3	−2.4	1.1	12.1	10.2
Ghana	1.2	4.6	3.5	4.4	−0.9	19.0	33.6
India	3.9	3.4	−0.5	−0.5	...	28.6	23.7
Mexico	0.9	1.1	0.2	−0.1	0.3	5.5	6.5
Morocco	5.6	5.0	−0.5	−1.1	0.6	25.2	18.7
Senegal	7.7	6.0	−1.7	−1.9	0.2	40.5	37.3
Thailand	3.9	3.4	−0.5	−1.0	0.5	26.2	18.2
Average	3.7	3.5	−0.2	−0.4	0.2	24.2	21.5
			Customs duties and other import taxes				
Bangladesh	3.2	2.7	−0.5	−0.3	−0.1	36.7	23.8
Chile	3.5	2.2	−1.3	−2.4	1.1	12.1	10.2
Ghana	0.7	3.1	2.4	2.1	0.3	11.9	22.4
India	3.9	3.3	−0.6	−0.6	...	28.5	23.2
Mexico	0.9	1.1	0.3	−0.1	0.4	5.4	6.5
Morocco	5.3	5.0	−0.2	−1.1	0.8	23.9	18.7
Senegal	7.6	6.0	−1.6	−1.8	0.3	39.9	37.3
Thailand	3.0	3.3	0.3	−0.3	0.6	20.0	18.0
Average	3.5	3.3	−0.1	−0.6	0.5	22.3	20.0
			Export and other international taxes				
Bangladesh	—	—	—	—	—	—	—
Chile	—	—	—	—	—	—	—
Ghana	0.4	1.6	1.1	2.4	−1.2	7.1	11.3
India	—	0.1	0.1	0.1	...	0.1	0.5
Mexico	—	—	—	—	—	0.1	—
Morocco	0.3	—	−0.3	—	−0.3	1.3	—
Senegal	0.1	—	−0.1	−0.1	−0.1	0.6	—
Thailand	0.9	—	−0.9	−0.8	−0.1	6.2	0.2
Average	0.2	0.2	—	0.2	−0.2	1.9	1.5

Sources: IMF, *Government Finance Statistics Yearbook* (various issues); and various IMF Staff Country Reports.

Appendix III   Summary of Tax Systems

This appendix presents in tabular form (Table 12) some of the basic features of the tax systems of the eight countries at various stages of their adjustment efforts.

Table 12. Summary of Tax Systems

Country	End of Preadjustment Period	End of First Adjustment Period	End of Second Adjustment Period
	Personal income tax rates		
Bangladesh	60% top rate, plus surcharge of 4.5%–9%; lowest rate first applies at 2.2 and highest at 111.0 times GDP per capita (GDPPC)	50% top rate; lowest rate at 1.4 and highest at 53.2 times GDPPC	25% top rate; lowest rate at 6.3 and highest at 30.7 times GDPPC; minimum tax of Tk 1,200 or Tk 1,800, with higher amount for the self-assessed
Chile	60% top rate; lowest rate at 1 Taxpayer Unit (TU; a monetary unit indexed to the consumer price index) (roughly 3 times GDPPC) and highest at 80 TUs	58% top rate; lowest positive rate at 10 TUs and highest at 100 TUs	Top rate 50%; lowest positive rate at 10 TUs and highest at 100 TUs
Ghana	60% top rate; lowest rate at 0.1 and highest at 1.9 times GDPPC	55% top rate; lowest rate at 0.3 and highest at 4.6 times GDPPC	50% top rate; lowest rate at 0.4 and highest at 12.6 times GDPPC
India	50% top rate, plus surcharge of 3%; lowest rate at 2.7 and highest at 15.3 times GDPPC	50% top rate, plus 6% surcharge; lowest rate at 2.4 and highest at 10.9 times GDPPC	
Mexico	55% top rate; lowest rate at 0.1 and highest at 29.3 times GDPPC	55% top rate; lowest rate at 0.1 and highest at 26.9 times GDPPC	35% top rate; lowest rate at 0.1 and highest at 7.3 times GDPPC; tax credit of 2.5% of tax due in higher brackets
Morocco	44% top rate, plus solidarity tax 4.4%, plus complementary tax at various rates of 1%–20%; highest rate at 47.0 times GDPPC	60% top rate, plus solidarity tax of up to 8.2%, plus complementary tax set at rate of 1%–18%; lowest rate at 1.0 and highest at 50.6 times GDPPC	48% top rate; lowest rate at 0.3 and highest at 6.3 times GDPPC; minimum turnover tax of 6% of gross income for some professionals and 0.5% for others
Senegal	75% top rate; lowest rate at 2.1 and highest at 103.6 times GDPPC	73% top rate; lowest rate at 1.5 and highest at 67.5 times GDPPC	64% top rate; lowest rate at 3.0 and highest at 63.2 times GDPPC
Thailand	65% top rate; lowest rate at 0.7 and highest at 73.4 times GDPPC	55% top rate; lowest rate at 0.6 and highest at 94.3 times GDPPC	37% top rate; lowest rate at 0.6 and highest at 76.1 times GDPPC
	Personal income tax base, and key structural features		
Bangladesh	Income from salary, interest, and dividends subject to withholding, with amount withheld from dividend income deductible from final tax obligations; dividend income up to Tk 5,000 (2 times GDPPC) subject to certain conditions is exempt; value of new or additional investments of up to the lesser of Tk 30,000 or 30% of the value of the new investment undertaken by the individual in designated industrial companies is deductible	Income from salary, interest, and dividends subject to withholding, with amount withheld from dividend income deductible from final tax obligations; bank interest up to Tk 15,000 and dividend income up to Tk 15,000 under certain circumstances are exempt (although taxed in the hands of the corporation making the distribution); new or additional investment of up to one-third of total income in designated industrial companies is deductible	Income from bank interest and dividends subject to withholding, with amount withheld for each of these deductible from final tax obligations; interest on government securities and dividend income up to Tk 30,000 are exempt (although taxed in the hands of the corporation making the distribution); new or additional investment of up to one-fifth of total income in designated industrial companies is deductible
Chile	Schedular element to tax system—schedular taxes at proportional rates on capital, labor, and professional income; tax on labor creditable against complementary income tax, IGC (a comprehensive income tax applying to all types of income, with exemptions essentially limited to personal and dependents' deductions); separate tax on capital gains	Major changes: indexation of tax brackets to TU; elimination of separate tax on capital gains; replacement of proportional tax on labor income by progressive tax, creditable against IGC	Major changes: tax on professional income eliminated; schedular tax on capital income creditable against complementary income tax; additional exemptions from complementary tax for contributions to various investment and saving schemes, including 100% of voluntary contributions to the account of the taxpayer with the national defined-contributions pension scheme

Table 12 (continued)

Personal income tax base, and key structural features (continued)

Country	End of Preadjustment Period	End of First Adjustment Period	End of Second Adjustment Period
Ghana	Taxable income includes income from virtually all sources, excluding that part of cash housing allowances that is below 20% of salary, rental income (which is separately assessed), income from cocoa, forestry and agricultural income for initial period of three to ten years, and interest on savings accounts; dividend income subject to final withholding at 15%	Basically unchanged from end of preadjustment period, except that dividend income now subject to tax, and, along with nonbank interest income subject to withholding at 30%, creditable against final tax liability	Basically unchanged from end of first period, except that dividends subject to a final withholding tax of 15%, and rental income no longer subject to a separate schedule
India	Income from all sources, excluding first Rs 10,000 (3 times GDPPC) of dividend income, an additional Rs 3,000 for dividend income from certain funds, and agricultural income (which is taxed at the state level); income tax obligations can be reduced by 20% of investments in certain forms of saving and equity instruments, with total deduction limited to Rs 10,000	Essentially unchanged from end of preadjustment period, though maximum deduction for investments raised to Rs 12,000	
Mexico	Income from all sources, excluding interest paid by savings banks and from some government bonds; dividend income subject to withholding at 55%, creditable against final tax liability, and interest income from bearer bonds at a final rate of 21%	Essentially the same as at the end of the preadjustment period, except that interest paid by savings banks and from some government bonds is now also subject to final withholding at 21%	As at the end of the first adjustment period, except that dividend distributions are neither subject to withholding nor taxed under the personal income tax; however, individuals may include dividend income to claim a credit for the corporate tax that has already been paid on such income; the final withholding taxes levied on bank interest and interest from government securities were lowered to 0%–2%
Morocco	A schedular system, with wage income subject to separate withholding taxes (the income tax and the national solidarity tax); the complementary income tax applies to all forms of income; dividends, interest earnings, and rental income are not subject to separate schedular taxes, but included in complementary tax base; dividend and interest income withheld at 25%, which at the taxpayer's option can be the final rate	Essentially unchanged from the end of the preadjustment period, except that agricultural income is exempt until the year 2000	Essentially unchanged from the end of the first period, except that dividend income now subject to 10%–30%; for both dividend and interest income the withholding tax at 15%, and interest income at withheld amount can be considered the final tax due or can be credited against personal income tax obligations
Senegal	A schedular system, with withholding taxes applying to wages and salaries, and dividends and nonbank interest (taxed at 8%–25%); a progressive tax with a top rate of 65% applies to all income	Essentially unchanged, except that dividends and nonbank interest taxed at 10%–25%, and the top rate of the comprehensive progressive income tax lowered to 60%	Essentially the same as at the end of the first period, except that dividends and nonbank interest now taxed at 8%–16%, with the top rate of the income tax lowered to 50%
Thailand	Income from all sources, except a part of dividend income varying from 25% to 35%; withholding tax on dividend income applies at the shareholder's personal income tax rate	Essentially unchanged from the end of the preadjustment period, except that individuals can exclude dividend income from their taxable income and pay the withholding tax, or include it and take a deduction of 30% of its value; certain interest subject to withholding at 15%, which is the final tax rate unless the individual chooses to have such income included as taxable income, whereupon the tax withheld is creditable	Essentially the same as at the end of the first adjustment period, except dividend income now subject to withholding at 10%; individuals can exclude such income from their taxable income or include it and take a deduction of 42% of its value

Company income tax rates

Bangladesh	30% for income below Tk 150,000 (75 times GDPPC), all income of public companies, and all income earned abroad and remitted to Bangladesh; otherwise 55%	Publicly traded industries, 45%; nonpublicly traded industries, 50%; all others, 60%; rebate of 10% of tax due for some income remitted from abroad to Bangladesh	Essentially unchanged, except that rates reduced as follows: for publicly traded companies, to 37.5%; for nonpublicly traded, to 42.5%; all others—including financial institutions—to 50%
Chile	General rate, 35%; banks and insurance companies, 40%	Subject to schedular tax on capital income at 10%, plus the "additional" tax of 40%	Major revisions to rate structure: earnings of resident companies, 15%; earnings of nonresident companies, 35% (with credit for corporate income tax already paid)
Ghana	Basic rate, 55%; companies producing excisable goods, 50%; mining income, and farming income following initial five-year exemption period, 45%; Ghanaian-owned companies for first five years of operations—reduced rates, 35%–45%; minimum turnover tax of 5% after initial five years, which is waived for mining and farming	Essentially unchanged	New rates as follows: basic rate (including farming after the exemption period), 35%; mining companies, 45%; banking, insurance, commerce, printing, and petroleum companies, 50%
India	Widely held Indian companies, 50%; closely held trading investment companies, 60%; other Indian companies, 55%; foreign companies (depending on type of income), up to 65%; surcharge of 5% of tax due for income above Rs 50,000 (8 times GDPPC); agricultural income taxed only at the state level	Rate changes as follows: widely held Indian companies, 45%; all closely held companies, 50%; surcharge of 15% of tax due for income above Rs 75,000 (8 times GDPPC)	
Mexico	5%–42% depending on profit level, with highest rate applicable for income above P 1,500,000 (11.2 times GDPPC)	11%–40%; new uniform base rate of 35% phased in from 1987 to 1991	34% for most companies; minimum profit tax of 2% of turnover after first two years of operation, credited against corporate income tax obligations
Morocco	40%–48% depending on profit level, plus solidarity tax of 4.0%–4.8%	Unchanged, except that forfeit (presumptive tax) based on turnover for small businesses introduced	General rate, 38% plus 3.8% solidarity tax; minimum turnover tax: standard rate, 0.5%; companies selling petroleum products, gas, butter, edible oils, flour, electricity, and water, 0.25%; minimum turnover tax creditable against corporate income tax obligations
Senegal	General rate (for industrial and commercial enterprises), 33⅓%; for unincorporated enterprises, 16%–28%; fixed-rate minimum tax of CFAF 400,000 for corporations, depending on size of turnover, which is creditable against corporate income tax obligations (income earned in the first two years of operations exempt)	Revised rates: unincorporated enterprises, 28%; fixed-rate minimum tax of CFAF 0.5–1 million	Revised rates: general rate, 35%; unincorporated enterprise income, 35%
Thailand	Public companies, 35%; nonpublic companies, 45%; petroleum companies, 50%	Revised rate: nonpublic companies, 30%; nonpublic companies, 35%	Revised rate: nonpublic companies, 30% (same as public)

Corporate income tax base, depreciation, and other key features

Bangladesh	All dividend income of companies taxed as ordinary corporate income at a rate of 30%, including that received from companies that enjoy tax holidays; depreciation rules quite liberal; operating losses from business activities can be carried forward for six years, and unutilized depreciation allowances for an indefinite period	Basically unchanged, except that all dividend income of companies now taxed at a final rate of 15%	Basically unchanged, except that dividend income received from tax-exempt companies is no longer taxable under certain conditions
Chile	Partial adjustment for inflation; straight-line depreciation	Major change: full indexation of balance sheet depreciation	Essentially unchanged

Table 12 (continued)

Corporate income tax base, depreciation, and other key features (continued)

Country	End of Preadjustment Period	End of First Adjustment Period	End of Second Adjustment Period
Ghana	Taxable income excludes dividends received from other companies; depreciation allowances vary—10%–20% for first year and 3%–15% a year thereafter depending on type of asset; losses not carried forward or backward, except for oil and farming enterprises; unutilized depreciation allowances can be carried forward; exempt: income from cocoa farming, income from farming for first five years of operation, income from some public enterprises	Essentially unchanged	Essentially unchanged
India	Net intercompany dividend payments are excluded from the tax base of the receiving company, provided that the dividend income received is in turn distributed by the receiving company (otherwise, dividend income is taxable for the receiving company); rates for depreciation vary at 5%–100%, depending on type of asset and business; losses can be carried forward for eight years under certain conditions (unutilized depreciation carried forward indefinitely)	Essentially unchanged	
Mexico	Dividend income received is subject to the corporate income tax but is deductible if then paid to another company (there is no withholding tax for dividends paid to another company); depreciation on straight-line basis varying at 5%–20%, depending on type of asset; losses may be carried back for one year or forward for four years	Interest income, the tax basis and cost of sales, and depreciation are inflation adjusted; provisions for treatment of dividends, basis of calculation of depreciation, and treatment of losses essentially unchanged	Essentially unchanged, except that dividend income paid out from past or current after-tax profit is neither subject to withholding nor taxed under the personal income tax; fixed assets are depreciated on a straight-line basis at 5%–25%, and at 50% for pollution-control equipment (for machinery and equipment, the entire present value can be taken in the first year); losses may be carried forward for five years, or up to ten years in certain circumstances
Morocco	Dividends included in the tax base; 85% deduction allowed on dividend income received from a corporation in which there is a 30% or more ownership by the receiving corporation; depreciation on straight-line basis; losses may be carried forward for five years (unutilized depreciation allowances may be carried forward indefinitely)	No major changes, except that dividend income from a company listed on the stock exchange and certain other entities is exempt; 5%–8% of taxable profit must by law be appropriated into approved investment vehicles, including purchase of government bonds; agricultural profits exempt until year 2000	No major changes, except that agricultural profits to be taxed at 18% after 2000, but cattle-raising companies exempt
Senegal	Depreciation usually straight-line at 3%–33%; losses may be carried forward for three years (unutilized depreciation allowances may be carried forward indefinitely)	Essentially unchanged	Essentially unchanged
Thailand	Intercompany dividend income received may be excluded from income tax base subject to a maximum of 15% of total company income; dividend income is subject to withholding; depreciation can be either straight-line 5%–100% or accelerated; losses can be carried forward for five years	Essentially unchanged; dividend income withholding rate 20%	Essentially unchanged; dividend income withholding rate 10%

	Corporate income tax holidays	
Bangladesh	Tax holidays may be granted for periods of five to nine years; special depreciation rules apply for new industrial undertakings (80%–100% write-off for property over the first two years), for companies with double or triple shifts (additional 50%–100% of normal depreciation deduction), and for ships other than those used for inland waterways (100% write-off over three years); special income tax rules and provisions for some agricultural earnings, for oil, gas, and mining companies, and for insurance and cooperative societies; some profits from the export of local goods, except for tea and jute, are tax exempt	Essentially unchanged, except that special rules for cooperatives no longer apply	Essentially unchanged, except that tax holidays for industrial, tourism, and export zones may be granted for periods of 5 to 12 years; an additional investment allowance applies for new industrial machinery; and special rules no longer apply to insurance companies
Chile	Numerous regional and sectoral incentives	Limited incentive schemes	No major change
Ghana	Various tax holidays may be granted, including holidays from income tax for up to five years (ten years for agricultural enterprises); exemption from customs duties on machinery imports; rebate of 30%–40% of corporate income tax and 30%–40% of customs duties for new plant and equipment for nonmetropolitan industries; manufacturing industries not including woodworking and metal processing entitled to 25%–50% income tax rebate if they export 5%–25% of production; additional 5%–10% allowance for depreciation for qualifying new plant and equipment used in an industrial establishment	Essentially unchanged, except that 30%–40% rebate of customs duties dropped	Essentially unchanged, except that rebates for manufacturing exporters range from 30% to 75%
India	Tax holiday from income tax for five years for new industrial undertakings within Free Trade Zones and for firms producing exports; limited income tax deductions for up to ten years for newly established manufacturing, hotel, and shipbuilding enterprises; most businesses may deduct up to 20% of profits if the money is used for plant and equipment or deposited with the Development Bank	Essentially unchanged, except that 20% profit deduction limited to tea producers	
Mexico	Accelerated depreciation on certain assets in any one of the first five years for firms located in priority zones; selective policy to promote new industrial activity in priority areas and employment generation, based on size, nature, and location of industrial activity (affects tourism, border areas, automobiles, non-oil exports); income tax rebates for publishers (50% of tax due) and agricultural, cattle, fishing, and forestry industries (25%–40% of tax due)	Essentially unchanged	Major changes as follows: selective promotion of new industrial activity limited to businesses along U.S. border and exporters (reduced benefits apply); accelerated depreciation provisions abolished
Morocco	Preferences for exporting and other designated firms include ten-year income tax holiday; other preferences can include preferential interest rates and depreciation profiles for real estate, housing, agriculture, and exports; some preferences are geographically based	Essentially unchanged	Changes as follows: income tax holiday for some exporting and other designated firms reduced to five years; for exporting firms a 50% tax rebate is given for following five years; exemption from import duties introduced

Table 12 (continued)

Country	End of Preadjustment Period	End of First Adjustment Period	End of Second Adjustment Period
		Corporate income tax holidays (continued)	
Senegal	Consumer cooperatives, mutual farm credit banks, and agricultural agencies exempt from income tax, while construction, printing, airlines, and maritime shipping exempt from minimum tax; temporary exemptions from income tax also available for new factories and for mining companies for five years; complete exemption from taxes and duties for companies in industrial free zone of Dakar; accelerated depreciation at twice normal first year rates for new machinery in manufacturing, transport, and farming; exemptions from import taxes and turnover tax for period of five to eight years for job-creating investment in manufacturing, agriculture, tourism, mining exploration, transport, telecommunications, and energy production	Essentially unchanged, except that: construction no longer exempt from minimum tax; tax credit of 50% of profit taxes for retained funds that are used for construction for industrial, tourism, and housing purposes for a period of up to eight years; narrowing of applicability of exemptions from import taxes and turnover tax (exemptions now related to location, size, use of technology, and use of local resources of firms investing in manufacturing, agriculture, tourism; maximum exemption period increased to 12 years)	Essentially unchanged
Thailand	Approved enterprises may be exempted from import and sales taxes on capital equipment, and for three to eight years on income taxes under the Investment Promotion Act	Essentially unchanged	Change in emphasis of incentive schemes from promotion of exports to regional development (encouraging location of industries outside Bangkok area); amount and type (by tax) of tax exemption varies, but can reach 100%; the period of exemption can reach eight years, depending on the region and type of export
		Domestic taxes on goods and services	
Bangladesh	Sales tax applying to certain specified domestically produced and imported manufactured items; rates imposed at 20% on some imported goods and domestically produced manufactured goods, 10% on industrial chemicals, processed food and furniture, and certain other goods if produced domestically	Essentially unchanged except that rate of 20% applies only to imports of manufactured goods	VAT introduced in 1991 and applied at the importer-manufacturer stage at a single rate of 15% (small firms, including those in the wholesale and retail sectors, pay a turnover tax of 2% unless they register for the VAT); exempt: cottage industries, textiles, foodstuffs, transport, insecticides, jute cuttings, oilseeds, some chemicals and drugs, fertilizers, basic plastics, some metal products; exports zero-rated
Chile	Cascading sales tax; exemptions: automobiles and certain other products (no provision for relief of tax embodied in inputs of taxed manufacturers); rates: 1%–70% (1969; most revenue from 8% rate)	VAT introduced in 1975 with general rate of 20%; initial exemptions for certain basic goods, reading materials, and special rates eliminated by 1980; exports zero-rated	Changes as follows: general rate, 18%; luxury rates, 30%–50%; alcohol, 13%–70%
Ghana	Single-stage sales tax on specified locally produced manufactured goods; rates: most goods not subject to an excise, 11.5%; goods subject to excises, 7.5%; salt, cigarettes, textiles, and certain building materials, 5%; imports, up to 30% (some specific); services tax on selected services: 25% for entertainment, 10% for hotels and restaurants; exempt: food, motor vehicles (which are subject to a special vehicle tax), education material, machinery and equipment for use in agriculture, manufacturing, and mining, petroleum products, one-band radio sets, and exports	Essentially unchanged, except that rate on most goods not subject to excise now 10%	Some changes in rate structure: general rate applying to both imports and domestically produced consumer goods of 17.5%; reduced rate of 7.5% for concession goods; 35%–100% for luxuries; all rates now ad valorem; some goods taxed at different rates

	Tax system	Changes	Recent changes
India	Modified VAT (Modvat) introduced in 1986/87: central excise duties on commodities used in the manufacture of 86 categories of goods are rebated if manufacturer subject to tax; textiles, petroleum, capital goods, and most services are not covered by the Modvat; sales taxes levied by the states are imposed on inter- and intrastate trade	Basically unchanged, except for addition of capital goods and petroleum to the list of taxable goods	
Mexico	VAT introduced in January 1980: general rate, 15%; some beverages, medicines, and production in the border and free-trade zones, 6%; luxury rate (for items such as caviar, some color televisions, motorcycles, golf equipment), 20%; zero-rated: exports, foodstuffs, some beverages, tractors; exempt: credit instruments, residential construction, banking services, education, newsprint	No major changes: reduced rate of 6% now applies to nonbasic processed foods and not to beverages; 20% applies to some services as well as luxury items; medical services added to exempt list	Major change: general rate 10%
Morocco	Turnover tax levied at production stage on manufactured goods at 4.2%–15%, and on services at 12%; many exemptions; rates can differ between imported and domestic goods	VAT introduced in 1986: general rate, 19%; transport, petroleum products, edible oils, tea and coffee, 7%; tourism services and banks, 12%; construction, 14%; luxury goods, 30%; exempt: agriculture and retail sector; small wholesalers and producers, basic foodstuffs and consumption goods such as bread, sugar, publications, and others; zero-rated: exports, unprocessed foodstuffs, and agricultural inputs; same rates for imports, but the list of exempted products can differ	Changes as follows: rate of 7% now applies to water, electricity, interest, financial services, and services of lawyers and doctors and no longer to tea and coffee; transport, tourism, bank services now taxed at 14%; the list of exempt basic foodstuffs expanded to include meat and fish; unprocessed foodstuffs no longer zero-rated; same rates for imports and domestic goods
Senegal	VAT applied at four rates on manufacturing, crafts, other productive activities: general rate, 20%; fuel oil, essential foodstuffs, various raw materials, 7%; other petroleum products, 34%; luxuries, 50%; services taxed at 7%–50%; exempt: agricultural production, wholesale and retail sectors, exports, activities of public entities, certain imports including crude oil	Essentially unchanged	Major change: elimination of the tax on services, except for a 15% tax on telecommunications
Thailand	Business tax on gross receipts of 12 categories of businesses, including importers; rates vary from 1.5% to 40%; certain other categories of businesses pay rates of between 0.5% and 10.5%; retailers generally exempt	Essentially unchanged	VAT introduced in 1992: single rate of 7%; exports zero-rated; turnover tax of 1.5% for small businesses and 2.5%–3% on "turnover" for financial services; exempt: agricultural products and inputs, education, domestic transport, newsprint, medical services

Excises

	Tax system	Changes	Recent changes
Bangladesh	Applied to a fairly large number of items—including jute, advertisements, electricity—in addition to traditional excisable products	Basic structure unchanged	Supplemental VAT applied at the producer level to the value added of 161 goods at 5%–350% (5% hotels, crude palm oil; 350% foreign cigarettes); additional specific rates on handmade cigarettes, textiles, and bank services; since no input credit allowed, the supplementary VAT operates essentially as an excise tax
Chile	Excises on traditional excisable products—tobacco and alcoholic beverages, petroleum—and a few others	Basic structure unchanged	
Ghana	Imposed on tobacco, alcohol, soap, and salt (at specific rates); on textiles, cosmetics, furniture, footwear, mineral water at ad valorem rates of 20%–60%; and on domestic cocoa sales at 100%	Basic structure unchanged, but maximum ad valorem rate for goods other than cocoa raised to 100%	Coverage of tax restricted to traditional excisable items—now including petroleum products—and cocoa sales

Table 12 (concluded)

Country	End of Preadjustment Period	End of First Adjustment Period	End of Second Adjustment Period
		Excises (continued)	
India	280 excises, with many specific rates; taxable goods include petroleum, tobacco, textiles, luxuries; maximum rate of 105%	Basic structure unchanged; maximum ad valorem rate lowered to 70%	
Mexico	In addition to traditional excisable goods (tobacco at 21%–140%, gasoline at 110%, alcohol at 15%–50%, petrochemical products at 13%–18%); a fairly large number of goods, including sugar, electricity, telephones, cement, cotton, chocolate, nonalcoholic beverages taxed at specific and ad valorem rates	Some nontraditional products dropped from the list; revised rates as follows: tobacco, 25%–180%; alcohol, 19%–50%; sugar, telephones, 32%–72%; nonalcoholic beverages, 16%–40%	Many excises abolished; revised rates as follows: alcohol, 21%–44%; tobacco, 21%–140%
Morocco	Numerous goods taxed, generally specific rates on alcohol, luxuries, petroleum, sugar; ad valorem rate on tobacco	Basic structure unchanged	Basic structure unchanged
Senegal	Moderately large number of goods subject to tax, including tobacco products, alcoholic beverages, edible oils, soft drinks, kola seeds, tea, and coffee, which are taxed at specific rates	Conversion of rate structure to 13 ad valorem rates; 150% for kola seeds; 36%–50% for alcohol; 27% tobacco; 2.5%–45% for beverages; 2.5% for cement	Basic structure unchanged
Thailand	Ad valorem excises imposed on beverages (20%–40%), tobacco (45%), cement and petroleum products (5%–41%); excises on certain other products are levied at specific rates	Revised rates as follows: beverages, 35%–50%; tobacco, 35%–48%; petroleum products, 5%–36%; cement taxed at 9%	Automobiles subject to tax at 32.5%–38%; revised rates as follows: beverages, 20%–48%; tobacco, up to 60%; petroleum products, 1%–36%; other luxuries, 2%–14%
		Export taxes	
Bangladesh	Three export taxes—on tea, hides, and raw jute	Raw jute no longer taxed	Only export tax is a specific tax on fish
Chile	None	None	None
Ghana	Four export taxes—rates at 5%–100% for lumber, logs, gold, and cocoa	Three export taxes—6%–100% for timber, gold, and cocoa	One export tax: 100% for cocoa receipts less producers' and marketing costs
India	No export taxes as such; 439 export controls	Fewer than 200 export controls, mainly on agricultural products	
Mexico	164 export taxes, mainly on agricultural products and petroleum; 55 commodity exports prohibited	62 taxed, mainly agricultural products and petroleum; and 39 prohibited	Most taxes and prohibitions eliminated; remaining apply mainly to agricultural products
Morocco	Several; phosphates and other minerals	Basic structure unchanged	Basic structure unchanged
Senegal	One export tax, on phosphates at 2.5%–5%	Basic structure unchanged	Basic structure unchanged
Thailand	Six export taxes; specific duties on hides and raw silk; ad valorem on rubber, rice, metal scraps, wood	Duties on rice and metal scraps eliminated	Duty on rubber eliminated
		Customs duties	
Bangladesh	Many rates; rates up to 125% on raw materials and semifinished goods, and up to 300% on finished goods; system of import licenses; many ad hoc exemptions	Basic structure unchanged	Substantial reduction in range of rates: 7.5% for basic inputs, 15% for raw materials, 30% for semifinished goods, 45% for consumption goods, and 60% for selected goods; concessional rates apply to spare parts, electrical equipment, agricultural inputs, and medicines

Chile	Numerous rates, 0%–220% plus; many goods subject to highest rates; widespread use of quantitative restrictions, simple average import duty at 94%	Major changes: uniform import tariff of 10%, except for motor vehicles and parts; quantitative restrictions eliminated; a few temporary tariffs on cars varying from 4% to 15% for 30 products	General rate of 15%, with 9% on imports to free zone, and 5% on boat engines and work tools for small fisheries; surcharge of 5%–15%; exempt: tax on imported capital can be deferred up to seven years
Ghana	Three ad valorem rates at 0%, 25%, and 30%; specific rates for food, live animals, beverages, tobacco, and textiles; use of quantitative restrictions; exempt: machinery, commercial vehicles, tractors, building material, some basic foodstuffs, and medicines	Changes: specific rates only on alcohol and tobacco; quantitative restrictions substantially liberalized; exemptions limited to agricultural machinery, tractors, crude oil, and medicines	Changes: four rates at 0%, 10%, 20%, and 25%; special tax of 10%–40% on textiles, beverages, and tobacco; some duties specific
India	Most imports subject to licensing; imports of consumer goods generally prohibited; wide dispersion of rates with maximum rate of 400%; ad hoc exemptions and reductions in rates	Liberalized; maximum tariff rate 100%; import licensing affects one-third of tariff lines; continued ad hoc exemptions and reductions in rates	
Mexico	Virtually all imports subject to licensing; rates up to 100%, though 90% of tariff lines have a duty rate less than 50%; certain primary and semiprocessed products and farm inputs enter duty-free	Relatively few imports subject to licensing; standardization of rates into seven bands ranging from 0%–40%	Further standardization of rates into three bands at 0%–20%
Morocco	Top rate of 400% (zero on imports of petroleum); restrictions apply to around two-thirds of imports; additional stamp duty tax of 10%; additional special import tax rate of 15% with many exemptions	Major changes: top rate reduced to 45%; additional special import tax rate reduced to 5%; quantitative restrictions replaced with tariffs	Major changes: top rate reduced to 40% (for certain agricultural products); additional 10% for capital goods imported by enterprises benefiting from investment codes; 12.5% for medicines; 15% for other imports
Senegal	Standard rate of 45%; special rate of 15% for countries with most-favored-nation treatment; special rate of 5% for trade with ECOWAS countries; additional fiscal duties at 10% (raw materials, capital goods), 40% (semifinished and noncompeting finished products), 50% (luxury products), and 75% (competing finished products); plus specific stamp duties; quantitative restrictions used; exempt: large number of products exempt from import taxes; essential foodstuffs, medicines, boats, and airplanes exempt from fiscal duty	Rate changes as follows: semifinished goods, 30%; luxury products, 35%; competing finished products, 65%; quantitative restrictions virtually abolished	Rate changes as follows: semifinished goods, 20%; luxury products, 30%; competing finished products, 50%; additional customs stamp duty of 3%
Thailand	Both specific and ad valorem rates; majority of goods assessed at rates from 10% to 80%; some goods subject to licensing; surcharges of 10%–30% imposed on 25 products	Basically unchanged	Seven rates: raw materials at 1%, primary goods and machinery at 5%, intermediate at 10%, finished goods at 20%, highly protected goods at 30%, motor vehicles at 42%–68.5%; exempt: lower rates for ASEAN Regional Trade Liberalization Area (around 1% of import value subject to nontariff barriers in agricultural and industrial sectors; additional surcharges can be imposed); also exempt: special policy goods, crude oil, fish, fertilizers, exports

Sources: Coopers and Lybrand, *International Tax Summaries* (various issues); Price Waterhouse, *Corporate and Individual Income Taxes: A Worldwide Summary* (various issues); and IMF staff data.
Note: Periods reflected in above tax summaries: end of preadjustment period—Bangladesh (March 1980), Chile (end of 1972), Ghana (September 1982), India (July 1991), Mexico (January 1983), Morocco (January 1980), Senegal (July 1983), Thailand (March 1980); end of first adjustment period—Bangladesh (July 1985), Chile (September 1982), Ghana (August 1986), India (July 1993), Mexico (August 1987), Morocco (January 1986), Senegal (July 1988), Thailand (August 1986); end of second adjustment period—Bangladesh (July 1994), Chile (end 1993), Ghana (July 1993), Mexico (July 1993), Morocco (January 1994), Senegal (July 1993), Thailand (July 1993).

References

Alesina, Alberto, and others, 1992, "Political Instability and Economic Growth, NBER Working Paper 4173 (Cambridge, Mass.: National Bureau of Economic Research, September).

Alesina, Alberto, and Roberto Perotti, 1996, "Fiscal Adjustments in OECD Countries: Composition and Macroeconomic Effects," Working Paper 96/70 (Washington: International Monetary Fund, July).

Amieva, Juan, 1991, "Public Social Expenditures, Labor Markets, and the Poor: The Mexican Experience, 1982–90" (unpublished, International Monetary Fund).

Bidani, Benu, and Martin Ravallion, 1995, "Decomposing Social Indicators Using Distributional Data," Policy Research Working Paper 1487 (Washington: World Bank, July).

Bovenberg, A. Lans, and others, 1989, "Tax Incentives and International Capital Flows: The Case of the United States and Japan," Working Paper 89/5 (Washington: International Monetary Fund, January).

Cashin, Paul, 1995, "Government Spending, Taxes, and Economic Growth," *Staff Papers,* International Monetary Fund, Vol. 42 (June), pp. 237–69.

Chirinko, Robert S., 1993, "Business Fixed Investment Spending: Modeling Strategies, Empirical Results, and Policy Implications," *Journal of Economic Literature,* Vol. 31 (December), pp. 1875–1911.

Chopra, Ajai, and others, 1995, *India: Economic Reform and Growth,* Occasional Paper 134 (Washington: International Monetary Fund, December).

Chua, Dale, 1995, "The Concept of Cost of Capital: Marginal Effective Tax Rate on Investment," in *Tax Policy Handbook,* ed. by Parthasarathi Shome (Washington: International Monetary Fund), pp. 161–65.

Coe, David T., and Elhanan Helpman, 1995, "International R&D Spillovers," *European Economic Review,* Vol. 39 (No. 5), pp. 859–87.

Denison, Edward F., 1962, *The Sources of Economic Growth and the Alternatives Before Us* (New York: Committee for Economic Development).

———, 1967, *Why Growth Rates Differ: Postwar Experience in Nine Western Countries* (Washington: Brookings).

Diamond, Peter, and Salvador Valdés-Prieto, 1994, "Social Security Reforms," in *The Chilean Economy: Policy Lessons and Challenges,* ed. by Barry P. Bosworth, Rudiger Dornbusch, and Raúl Labán (Washington: Brookings).

Easterly, William R., and Sergio Rebelo, 1993, "Fiscal Policy and Economic Growth: An Empirical Investigation," NBER Working Paper 4499 (Cambridge, Mass.: National Bureau of Economic Research).

Feldstein, Martin, 1974, "Social Security, Induced Retirement, and Aggregate Capital Accumulation," *Journal of Political Economy,* Vol. 82 (September), pp. 905–26.

———, 1994, "Fiscal Policies, Capital Formation, and Capitalism," NBER Working Paper 4885 (Cambridge, Mass.: National Bureau of Economic Research, March).

———, 1995, "Social Security and Saving: New Time-Series Evidence," NBER Working Paper 5054 (Cambridge, Mass.: National Bureau of Economic Research, March).

Feltenstein, Andrew, and Jiming Ha, 1995, "The Role of Infrastructure in Mexican Economic Reform," *World Bank Economic Review,* Vol. 9 (May), pp. 287–304.

Galal, Ahmed, and Mary Shirley, eds., 1994, *Does Privatization Deliver?* (Washington: World Bank, March).

Gerson, Philip R., forthcoming, "The Impact of Fiscal Policy Variables on Output Growth," Working Paper (Washington: International Monetary Fund).

Ghana, Ministry of Finance, 1994, *Public Expenditure Review 1993* (Accra, April).

Goldsbrough, David, and others, 1996, *Reinvigorating Growth in Developing Countries: Lessons from Adjustment Policies in Eight Economies,* Occasional Paper 139 (Washington: International Monetary Fund, July).

Graham, Carol, 1994, *Safety Nets, Politics, and the Poor: Transitions to Market Economies* (Washington: Brookings).

Hachette, Dominique, and Rolf Lüders, 1993, *Privatization in Chile: An Economic Appraisal* (San Francisco: ICS).

Hadjimichael, Michael, and others, 1996, *Adjustment for Growth: The African Experience,* Occasional Paper 143 (Washington: International Monetary Fund, October).

Happe, Nancy, and John Wakeman-Linn, 1994, "Military Expenditure and Arms Trade: Alternative Data Sources," Working Paper 94/69 (Washington: International Monetary Fund, June).

Haque, Nadeem Ul, and Ratna Sahay, 1996, "Do Government Wage Cuts Close Budget Deficits? A Conceptual Framework for Developing Countries and Transition Economies," Working Paper 96/19 (Washington: International Monetary Fund).

Harberger, Arnold C., 1988, "Reflections on Uniform Taxation," paper presented at the 44th Congress of the International Institute of Public Finance, Istanbul, August.

Holzmann, Robert, 1996, "Pension Reform, Financial Market Development, and Economic Growth: Preliminary Evidence from Chile," Working Paper 96/94 (Washington: International Monetary Fund, August).

International Monetary Fund, 1995a, *Social Dimensions of the IMF's Policy Dialogue* (prepared by IMF staff for World Summit for Social Development, Copenhagen, March 6–12, 1995), Pamphlet Series, No. 47 (Washington).

———, Fiscal Affairs Department, 1995b, *Unproductive Public Expenditures: A Pragmatic Approach to Policy Analysis,* Pamphlet Series, No. 48 (Washington).

———, 1996, *World Economic Outlook* (Washington, October).

Kochhar, Kalpana, and others, 1996, *Thailand: The Road to Sustained Growth,* Occasional Paper 146 (Washington: International Monetary Fund, December).

Leechor, Chad, 1994, "Ghana: Frontrunner in Adjustment," in *Adjustment in Africa: Lessons from Country Case Studies,* ed. by Ishrat Husain and Rashid Faruqee (Washington: World Bank).

McDermott, John, and Robert Wescott, 1996, "An Empirical Analysis of Fiscal Adjustments," Working Paper 96/59 (Washington: International Monetary Fund, June).

Mackenzie, G.A., and Peter Stella, 1996, *Quasi-Fiscal Operations of Public Financial Institutions,* Occasional Paper 142 (Washington: International Monetary Fund).

Mackenzie, G.A., and others, forthcoming, *Pension Regimes and Saving,* Occasional Paper (Washington: International Monetary Fund).

Meller, Patricio, 1992, *Adjustment and Equity in Chile* (Paris: Development Centre, Organization for Economic Cooperation and Development).

Mendoza, E.G., G.M. Milesi-Ferretti, and P. Asea, 1995, "Do Taxes Matter for Long-Run Growth? Harberger's Superneutrality Conjecture," Working Paper 95/79 (Washington: International Monetary Fund, August).

Morrisson, Christian, 1991, *Adjustment and Equity in Morocco* (Paris: Development Centre, Organization for Economic Cooperation and Development).

New Zealand, State Services Commission, 1993, "Decision-Making in New Zealand Government," ed. by J.R. Nethercote, Brian Galligan, and Cliff Walsh (Wellington); prepared by the Federalism Research Centre, Australian National University, in association with the Institute of Policy Studies, Victoria University of Wellington, and the New Zealand State Services Commission.

Nunberg, Barbara, and John Nellis, 1995, "Civil Service Reform and the World Bank," Discussion Paper 161 (Washington: World Bank).

Psacharopoulos, George, 1994, "Returns to Investment in Education: A Global Update," *World Development,* Vol. 22 (September), pp. 1325–43.

Roe, Alan, and Hartmut Schneider, 1992, *Adjustment and Equity in Ghana* (Paris: Development Centre, Organization for Economic Cooperation and Development).

Rouis, Mustapha, 1994, "Senegal: Stabilization, Partial Adjustment, and Stagnation," in *Adjustment in Africa: Lessons from Country Case Studies,* ed. by Ishrat Husain and Rashid Faruqee (Washington: World Bank).

Sala-i-Martin, Xavier, 1992, "Public Welfare and Growth," Discussion Paper 666 (New Haven, Conn.: Yale University, Economic Growth Center, June).

———, 1996, "Transfers, Social Safety Nets, and Economic Growth," Working Paper 96/40 (Washington: International Monetary Fund).

Schadler, Susan, and others, 1995, *IMF Conditionality: Experience Under Stand-By and Extended Arrangements—Part I: Key Issues and Findings,* Occasional Paper 128 (Washington: International Monetary Fund).

Smith, Roger S., 1990, "Factors Affecting Saving, Policy Tools, and Tax Reform: A Review," *Staff Papers,* International Monetary Fund, Vol. 37 (March), pp. 1–70.

Stotsky, Janet, 1995, "Summary of IMF Tax Policy Advice," in *Tax Policy Handbook,* ed. by Parthasarathi Shome (Washington: International Monetary Fund), pp. 279–83.

Tanzi, Vito, ed., 1984, *Taxation, Inflation, and Interest Rates* (Washington: International Monetary Fund, 1984).

———, 1989, "Fiscal Policy, Growth, and the Design of Stabilization Programs," in *Fiscal Policy, Stabilization, and Growth in Developing Countries,* ed. by Mario I. Blejer and Ke-young Chu (Washington: International Monetary Fund).

Tanzi, Vito, and Parthasarathi Shome, 1993, "A Primer on Tax Evasion," *Staff Papers,* International Monetary Fund, Vol. 40 (December), pp. 807–28.

United States, Office of Management and Budget, 1995, *Appendix—Budget of the United States Government, Fiscal Year 1996* (Washington: U.S. Government Printing Office).

van de Walle, Dominique, 1994, "The Distribution of Subsidies through Public Health Services in Indonesia, 1978–87," *World Bank Economic Review,* Vol. 8, pp. 279–309.

Velasco, Andrés, 1994, "The State and Economic Policy: Chile 1952–92," in *The Chilean Economy: Policy Lessons and Challenges,* ed. by Barry P. Bosworth, Rudiger Dornbusch, and Raúl Labán (Washington: Brookings).

Wheeler, Christopher W., Stephen Raudenbush, and Aida Pasigna, 1989, "Policy Initiatives to Improve Primary School Quality in Thailand: An Essay on Implementation, Constraints, and Opportunities for Educational Improvement," BRIDGES Research Report Series, No. 5 (Cambridge, Mass.: BRIDGES [Basic Research and Implementation in Developing Education Systems], June).

World Bank, 1990, *World Development Report 1990: Poverty* (New York: Oxford University Press).

———, 1991a, *Decision and Change in Thailand: Three Studies in Support of the Seventh Plan* (Washington, July).

————, 1991b, *Lessons of Tax Reform* (Washington).

————, 1992a, *Adjustment Lending and Mobilization of Private and Public Resources for Growth,* Policy and Research Series, No. 22 (Washington).

————, 1992b, *Republic of Ghana: Public Expenditure Review, 1992–94* (Washington, September).

————, 1993a, *World Development Report 1993: Investing in Health* (New York: Oxford University Press).

————, 1993b, *Senegal: Public Expenditure Review* (Washington, May).

————, 1994a, *Mexico: Second Primary Education Project* (Washington, March).

————, 1994b, *World Development Report 1994* (New York: Oxford University Press).

————, 1994c, *Kingdom of Morocco: Public Expenditure—Issues and Outlook* (Washington, August).

————, 1995a, *Bureaucrats in Business: The Economics and Politics of Government Ownership* (New York: Oxford University Press).

————, 1995b, "India: Recent Economic Developments and Prospects" (Washington).

Recent Occasional Papers of the International Monetary Fund

149. The Composition of Fiscal Adjustment and Growth: Lessons from Fiscal Reforms in Eight Economies, by G.A. Mackenzie, David W.H. Orsmond, and Philip R. Gerson. 1997.

148. Nigeria: Experience with Structural Adjustment, by Gary Moser, Scott Rogers, and Reinold van Til, with Robin Kibuka and Inutu Lukonga. 1997.

147. Aging Populations and Public Pension Schemes, by Sheetal K. Chand and Albert Jaeger, 1996.

146. Thailand: The Road to Sustained Growth, by Kalpana Kochhar, Louis Dicks-Mireaux, Balazs Horvath, Mauro Mecagni, Erik Offerdal, and Jianping Zhou. 1996.

145. Exchange Rate Movements and Their Impact on Trade and Investment in the APEC Region, by Takatoshi Ito, Peter Isard, Steven Symansky, and Tamim Bayoumi. 1996.

144. National Bank of Poland: The Road to Indirect Instruments, by Piero Ugolini. 1996.

143. Adjustment for Growth: The African Experience, by Michael T. Hadjimichael, Michael Nowak, Robert Sharer, and Amor Tahari. 1996.

142. Quasi-Fiscal Operations of Public Financial Institutions, by G.A. Mackenzie and Peter Stella. 1996.

141. Monetary and Exchange System Reforms in China: An Experiment in Gradualism, by Hassanali Mehran, Marc Quintyn, Tom Nordman, and Bernard Laurens. 1996.

140. Government Reform in New Zealand, by Graham C. Scott. 1996.

139. Reinvigorating Growth in Developing Countries: Lessons from Adjustment Policies in Eight Economies, by David Goldsbrough, Sharmini Coorey, Louis Dicks-Mireaux, Balazs Horvath, Kalpana Kochhar, Mauro Mecagni, Erik Offerdal, and Jianping Zhou. 1996.

138. Aftermath of the CFA Franc Devaluation, by Jean A.P. Clément, with Johannes Mueller, Stéphane Cossé, and Jean Le Dem. 1996.

137. The Lao People's Democratic Republic: Systemic Transformation and Adjustment, edited by Ichiro Otani and Chi Do Pham. 1996.

136. Jordan: Strategy for Adjustment and Growth, edited by Edouard Maciejewski and Ahsan Mansur. 1996.

135. Vietnam: Transition to a Market Economy, by John R. Dodsworth, Erich Spitäller, Michael Braulke, Keon Hyok Lee, Kenneth Miranda, Christian Mulder, Hisanobu Shishido, and Krishna Srinivasan. 1996.

134. India: Economic Reform and Growth, by Ajai Chopra, Charles Collyns, Richard Hemming, and Karen Parker with Woosik Chu and Oliver Fratzscher. 1995.

133. Policy Experiences and Issues in the Baltics, Russia, and Other Countries of the Former Soviet Union, edited by Daniel A. Citrin and Ashok K. Lahiri. 1995.

132. Financial Fragilities in Latin America: The 1980s and 1990s, by Liliana Rojas-Suárez and Steven R. Weisbrod. 1995.

131. Capital Account Convertibility: Review of Experience and Implications for IMF Policies, by staff teams headed by Peter J. Quirk and Owen Evans. 1995.

130. Challenges to the Swedish Welfare State, by Desmond Lachman, Adam Bennett, John H. Green, Robert Hagemann, and Ramana Ramaswamy. 1995.

129. IMF Conditionality: Experience Under Stand-By and Extended Arrangements. Part II: Background Papers. Susan Schadler, Editor, with Adam Bennett, Maria Carkovic, Louis Dicks-Mireaux, Mauro Mecagni, James H.J. Morsink, and Miguel A. Savastano. 1995.

128. IMF Conditionality: Experience Under Stand-By and Extended Arrangements. Part I: Key Issues and Findings, by Susan Schadler, Adam Bennett, Maria Carkovic, Louis Dicks-Mireaux, Mauro Mecagni, James H.J. Morsink, and Miguel A. Savastano. 1995.

127. Road Maps of the Transition: The Baltics, the Czech Republic, Hungary, and Russia, by Biswajit Banerjee, Vincent Koen, Thomas Krueger, Mark S. Lutz, Michael Marrese, and Tapio O. Saavalainen. 1995.

126. The Adoption of Indirect Instruments of Monetary Policy, by a staff team headed by William E. Alexander, Tomás J.T. Baliño, and Charles Enoch. 1995.

125. United Germany: The First Five Years—Performance and Policy Issues, by Robert Corker, Robert A. Feldman, Karl Habermeier, Hari Vittas, and Tessa van der Willigen. 1995.

124. Saving Behavior and the Asset Price "Bubble" in Japan: Analytical Studies, edited by Ulrich Baumgartner and Guy Meredith. 1995.

123. Comprehensive Tax Reform: The Colombian Experience, edited by Parthasarathi Shome. 1995.

122. Capital Flows in the APEC Region, edited by Mohsin S. Khan and Carmen M. Reinhart. 1995.

121. Uganda: Adjustment with Growth, 1987–94, by Robert L. Sharer, Hema R. De Zoysa, and Calvin A. McDonald. 1995.

120. Economic Dislocation and Recovery in Lebanon, by Sena Eken, Paul Cashin, S. Nuri Erbas, Jose Martelino, and Adnan Mazarei. 1995.

119. Singapore: A Case Study in Rapid Development, edited by Kenneth Bercuson with a staff team comprising Robert G. Carling, Aasim M. Husain, Thomas Rumbaugh, and Rachel van Elkan. 1995.

118. Sub-Saharan Africa: Growth, Savings, and Investment, by Michael T. Hadjimichael, Dhaneshwar Ghura, Martin Mühleisen, Roger Nord, and E. Murat Uçer. 1995.

117. Resilience and Growth Through Sustained Adjustment: The Moroccan Experience, by Saleh M. Nsouli, Sena Eken, Klaus Enders, Van-Can Thai, Jörg Decressin, and Filippo Cartiglia, with Janet Bungay. 1995.

116. Improving the International Monetary System: Constraints and Possibilities, by Michael Mussa, Morris Goldstein, Peter B. Clark, Donald J. Mathieson, and Tamim Bayoumi. 1994.

115. Exchange Rates and Economic Fundamentals: A Framework for Analysis, by Peter B. Clark, Leonardo Bartolini, Tamim Bayoumi, and Steven Symansky. 1994.

114. Economic Reform in China: A New Phase, by Wanda Tseng, Hoe Ee Khor, Kalpana Kochhar, Dubravko Mihaljek, and David Burton. 1994.

113. Poland: The Path to a Market Economy, by Liam P. Ebrill, Ajai Chopra, Charalambos Christofides, Paul Mylonas, Inci Otker, and Gerd Schwartz. 1994.

112. The Behavior of Non-Oil Commodity Prices, by Eduardo Borensztein, Mohsin S. Khan, Carmen M. Reinhart, and Peter Wickham. 1994.

111. The Russian Federation in Transition: External Developments, by Benedicte Vibe Christensen. 1994.

110. Limiting Central Bank Credit to the Government: Theory and Practice, by Carlo Cottarelli. 1993.

109. The Path to Convertibility and Growth: The Tunisian Experience, by Saleh M. Nsouli, Sena Eken, Paul Duran, Gerwin Bell, and Zühtü Yücelik. 1993.

108. Recent Experiences with Surges in Capital Inflows, by Susan Schadler, Maria Carkovic, Adam Bennett, and Robert Kahn. 1993.

107. China at the Threshold of a Market Economy, by Michael W. Bell, Hoe Ee Khor, and Kalpana Kochhar with Jun Ma, Simon N'guiamba, and Rajiv Lall. 1993.

106. Economic Adjustment in Low-Income Countries: Experience Under the Enhanced Structural Adjustment Facility, by Susan Schadler, Franek Rozwadowski, Siddharth Tiwari, and David O. Robinson. 1993.

105. The Structure and Operation of the World Gold Market, by Gary O'Callaghan. 1993.

104. Price Liberalization in Russia: Behavior of Prices, Household Incomes, and Consumption During the First Year, by Vincent Koen and Steven Phillips. 1993.

103. Liberalization of the Capital Account: Experiences and Issues, by Donald J. Mathieson and Liliana Rojas-Suárez. 1993.

Note: For information on the title and availability of Occasional Papers not listed, please consult the IMF Publications Catalog or contact IMF Publication Services.